Letters from Constance

MARY HOCKING

Published by VIRAGO PRESS Limited, 1992
20–23 Mandela Street, Camden Town, London NW1 0HQ

First published in Britain by Chatto & Windus 1991

The lines from 'Fern Hill' by Dylan Thomas on pp. 111–112
are from *Collected Poems* and are reproduced by
permission of J. M. Dent

The lines by Jean-Pierre de Caussade are from
The Flame of Divine Love (Darton Longman & Todd, 1984),
arranged by Robert Llewellyn, © The Julian Shrine

*A CIP catalogue record for this book
is available from the British Library*

Printed in Great Britain by
Cox & Wyman Ltd., Reading, Berkshire

Dear James,

These are the letters Linnie sent to me. When we could see that a time might come when someone would say, 'Has anyone done Sheila Douglas?' it was agreed that I should destroy all her letters to me. I had not realised she had kept so many of mine.

Sheila was one of those highly intelligent people who are unable to come to terms with the telephone – a disability which I sometimes think altered our lives. Whenever one phoned her it was sure to be the wrong moment. At best, she was stilted; at worst, abrupt and uncommunicative. She was, however, adept at letters of apology, explaining that she had been in the garden, the bath, hair-washing, plucking a chicken, sickening for 'flu. . . So, in place of the trivialities people so often exchange over the telephone, we wrote letters.

There was other correspondence relating to our friendship and I still have two postcards I sent to my parents not long before my father died. I found them marking a place in my mother's Bible. They give no address and are undated, but I know that the year was 1933 and the place a guide camp. Both are commendably brief. The first: 'I don't like it here. Please come quickly and take me home.' The second: 'A girl called Sheila Douglas and I had a nice walk by a stream and Joyce Pillinger fell in. Can I stay until the end of the week, please?'

The next term Sheila and I were in the same form at school. She had three brothers and through her, I, an only child, was introduced to the rough and tumble of sibling rivalry. After my father died, her parents treated me as though I were a member of the family who just happened to live several streets away. This attitude was a revelation to me as my mother insisted that people pass tests of her own devising before gaining entry to our house. Mr Douglas worked on the *Methodist Recorder* and was a lay preacher. He believed that all should be welcome in his home and Mrs Douglas cheerfully dealt with the consequences, of which I was the most long-lasting. From then until we left school Sheila and I were hardly ever apart. There was a time, after the war, when it seemed we should live in close proximity, but all that changed and there were many years when we saw each other infrequently. So there are a lot of letters.

I have not the heart to destroy them. I shall leave them to you, dear James, because yours are the safest hands.

November, 1990

Dear absent one,

How I missed you on the great occasion of our school leaving. I so longed to catch your eye while old Addiscombe delivered her peroration, swathed in deep crimson with two inches of black slip showing, putting me in mind of those lines from that grim hymn – 'Wherefore red is thine apparel/Like the Conquerors of earth/And arrayed like those who carol/O'er the reeking vineyard's mirth . . .'.

And what, do I hear you ask, were the thoughts we were to take out into the great world with us? Or perhaps you think, being absent, you should be spared the knowledge? I remember Daddy once said of a patient that he died of lack of interest in life and the only thing which could have captured his attention was his funeral. You are more fortunate, not only in not having died, but in having a faithful observer to record the tributes paid to you.

So, imagine us all assembled in the hall, exhilarated by the thought that this occasion would never repeat itself, because even those who were not leaving were likely to be evacuated.

'For all of us here, life will never be the same again,' she began. She does have a way of saying these things which puts a damper on exhilaration. It wasn't a bright day and the hall seemed cavernous. Cissie Parker looked positively desolate and I certainly had that 'doomed generation' feeling I always get when I read those books about soldiers knee-deep in Flanders mud, to say nothing of self-pity. But she soon moved briskly to the matter of our bearing in time of adversity and expressed the hope that the lessons learnt at school would carry us through whatever hazards might await us. The hazards she had in mind were moral – I don't think she minded about our being blown up so long as we were intact before that. 'It is not bombs which will destroy you, the destroyer is within . . .', and much more in the same vein.

You may wonder where you come into this and I'm not surprised, since you haven't shown much sign of burgeoning into the St Joan of Ealing Common. But . . . 'There is one of our number, though not among us today, who has expressed in action virtues to which so often we give only lip service. A small act, perhaps, when measured against the deeds which concern us at this troubled time, yet an act which gives an example of hope and courage to us all.

'Sheila Douglas left school a week ago to join her family in what might be their last holiday together, all three of her brothers being in the Territorial Army. Last Saturday, Sheila was on the beach at Newquay. It was early morning and she had gone for a walk on her own. There were only two other people on the beach – a young woman and a small boy. The child, perhaps not wisely advised by his mother, insisted on paddling. This is the Atlantic Ocean and even when it is not dangerously rough, it is boisterous. He was soon borne beyond his depth. The distraught mother waded into the breakers; but she could not swim and must have watched her child drown had it not been for Sheila, who immediately cast off her frock and swam towards the child, calling to the mother to get help. The place was unfrequented at this hour and it was over fifteen minutes before help arrived. An act of courage on the spur of the moment is something of which we might all be capable. This, however, was a sustained struggle which Sheila must have known might put her own life at risk. It is hard to fight the sea on one's own, desperately hard when buoying up another. Indeed, with that strong tide, had she not managed to cling to a rock, both she and the boy would undoubtedly have been swept out to sea and drowned. She clung there tenaciously. But as the minutes passed and the waves broke around her, the thought must have crossed her mind that the sea would win and eventually the rock would be submerged. [But the tide was going out, surely? Oh, how hard of heart is your friend Constance to think such a thought at such a time.] She is now in hospital, shocked, bruised and lacerated, but happily expected to make a complete recovery.

'She is, as we all know, a very strong swimmer. It would not be advisable for any girl not so well-equipped to emulate her action. The wise course [gazing at us who were less than dolphins with some severity] would be to run for help. To plunge in heedlessly would merely place an extra burden on rescuers. Never act impetuously if you are not equipped to achieve your aim. But, should it ever fall to you to act as Sheila Douglas acted, remember that as well as courage and generosity of spirit, you may need the tenacity to hold on.'

As you can imagine, it was all we could do to hold on to sobriety as we listened, knowing you would have found it so hilarious you would have been ordered to leave the hall.

This was your day. My mother had come to see old Addiscombe. I never can persuade her to give up hoping for academic success for me. She feels she owes it to Daddy's memory to squeeze every opportunity dry. According to her, she said – and I squirm as I write this – 'If Sheila Douglas can get into Cambridge, I can't understand why Constance shouldn't be accepted. After all, her father was a doctor.'

The reply, which I hope pleases you, was 'Sheila Douglas is a quite exceptionally gifted girl for whom we have great hopes. One of her poems has been commended by Walter de la Mare, who is a friend of the Chairman of the Governors.' Later in the conversation, she said, and one can imagine the glacial smile which accompanied the words, 'Constance is amusing, but she has no mind. She will get married.'

Before I left, I had a session with Miss Tobin, who has rather different ideas about my ability. She thought I should consider university – though not, of course, Oxford or Cambridge. 'I feel there are qualities we have failed to bring out in you.' I think she really believes she has failed, the dear thing. She is the only member of staff who has ever tried with me and I felt mean for not having helped more. 'You are more than competent at English. It would be sad if you did not develop this gift. You would have to work very hard, but I think you would be capable of getting a good degree. It is only too easy to settle for second best, Constance. I know you have felt rather lost since your father died, but you should have got over that by now. You still take refuge in playing the jester. Your friend Sheila may seem to you as much a humorist as you are yourself; but have you never noticed how much sharper and more questioning is her mind? She will leave you far behind if you are not careful and I know that would upset you. You like to give the impression of being indifferent, but I believe you really do care quite a lot what people think of you. Be sure you give them something worthwhile to think about.'

So, I leave school potentially a moral and intellectual failure while you trail clouds of glory, in spite of being much naughtier than I ever was. I suppose the difference is that yours is the kind of naughtiness that the staff see as going with a questioning mind. And then, you had a nice way of seeming to invite them to play your game. I never could get on those terms with them.

Should all this talk of intellectual prowess lead you to imagine yourself growing into an old, unloved bluestocking, let me tell you about the class photograph. There you all are, bunched tight as cauliflower florets, while I rise above you not in the least like the golden sunflower you so kindly said I resembled, but some poor weedy thing which has outgrown its strength. I look down rather queasily, while you stare straight at the camera – right into its innards, as if you expected it to be Masefield's box of delights. I showed the photograph to our curate, of whom I had such hopes, and he pointed to you and said, 'Who is that one?' I said, 'She is small and stunted with a snub nose and a hideous amount of freckles.' He said, 'It's a real face' as if the rest of us were only half formed owing to some hitch in the developing process.

Did I say that Miss Addiscombe thinks war is inevitable? Not one of her more original ideas, what with all the sandbags outside the town hall and gas masks being issued.

After I had cleared my desk I walked home across the Common with Joyce Pillinger and it seemed like any other day. She told me that Margery Harris is having to get married. Margery Harris! You wouldn't think Cupid's dart could find its way into that lump.

Will you be home soon? I don't relish giving a day-to-day account of how Ealing went to war, even if my English is more than competent.

I'm trying to get particulars about the WRNS without Mummy's knowing. She believes that in the Great War the Naafi tea tasted so foul because something was put in it to quieten the sailors' sexual urges.

If you aren't home by Saturday, I will write again.

Yours with a bow and a smile,
Constance

Education Office
November, 1939

Dear Sheila,

The time is the lunch hour; the place, the reception room of an education office somewhere in the outer reaches of Middlesex. Only one character: a haggard young woman, left in charge of a switchboard she has not yet mastered. It is foggy outside, but one can just discern an overgrown garden in which dim figures are engaged in stirrup pump practice. A chill feeling of hopelessness seeps into the room, which is cold because the County Council sees it as part of its war effort to ensure that its staff are finished off by consumption before the Germans get a crack at them.

I miss you so much. No one here has a sense of humour. The Education Officer fusses about staffing ratios, fuel rationing and the quality of toilet paper now supplied to schools. He has an endless capacity for anxiety and the other men (three in all) are little better, worrying about what arrangements to make for their families when they are called up. The girls' talk is all about soldiers and they think I am stuck-up because I don't join in; whereas I am only silent because I haven't got a soldier. I knew that sooner or later the deficiencies in our education would make themselves felt.

Your favourite brother, John, blessings on the dear lad, took me to coffee at Zeeta's on Saturday. He was quite the most presentable man in the room and almost won me over to the Army: but then John would grace any uniform he wore and the wonder is that he is unaware of it. I felt a bit of a fool with him. When I talk to a man I do it for effect, but John listens as if the talk matters. This is disconcerting as I haven't anything to say which will bear the weight of serious examination. Perhaps I could learn if I put my mind to it; but I seem to remember there was something going on with Jill Pryce at one time. Do you know if it's serious? I wouldn't want to poach.

I was so pleased to get your letter. I had been a bit afraid you might not find the time to write, such exciting things are happening to you. I enjoyed your description of your tutor's family, talking over breakfast about Wordsworth and Coleridge as if they were personally acquainted with them and exchanging malicious jokes at their expense. You say you find the family daunting. Have no fear, you will soon come up with appropriate jokes of your own. Remember you have the advantage of being a very strong swimmer; quite strong enough to stay afloat in that little pond.

Pause while I manhandle the switchboard and take a message about dwindling fuel stocks. He spoke so fast I didn't get the name of the school. I must try to sort this out; but how – other than telephoning all the schools, of which there are forty-eight in this division?

I leave you to the higher realms inhabited by Wordsworth and Coleridge.

Yours from the nether regions,
Constance

My poor Sheila,

How are you to keep up a correspondence with anyone whose life is so dull? Nothing of note has happened since Christmas. When shall we have such walks and talks again? For the present, you will have to be content with the unnoteworthy.

It seems early in life to start looking back on the good old days, but, although at the time I thought it an awful fag, I now realise how lucky we were to be within walking distance of school. I am hagridden by transport problems. My day begins with a ten-minute walk to the station. If I, or the train, happen to be late, I miss my connection at Richmond. Even when it isn't freezing outside, the temperature in the office is zero on the occasions when I arrive late and the thaw doesn't set in until after lunch. So, quite often, the only part of the day which is free of bad feeling of one kind or another is between two and four in the afternoon. After four, as I wash up the tea things (I also make the tea), I start to worry about whether I shall be able to leave in time to catch my train. If I don't make the connection at Richmond I shall be an hour late home and Mummy will have convinced herself that I have been knocked down in the blackout. On the days when the Education Officer doesn't begin to look at the post until the time we are due to leave, it does not occur to any of my fellow workers, all of whom live locally, to say that I can go. All must be in attendance for the sticking down of envelopes and application of stamps. Then, since I am the most junior, I must be the one to take any parcels to the post office. Never a day passes, but there is at least one parcel. Imagine me as I set out for the post office, burden clasped to thin breast, anxious face shadow-blotched in moonlight, a gaunt, scurrying figure cast upon the uncaring streets, not unlike one of the more ill used of Dickens's heroines – except that they are so nauseously accepting of their fate while I am full of hatred.

Mummy doesn't want me to leave because at the end of a

lifetime of service I shall be rewarded with a local government pension. She never thought about money before Daddy died; now she thinks of little else. However, there is a glimmer of light. As I am so demonstrably miserable, she has conceded that when I have been at the wretched place long enough to have established myself in the regard of the Education Officer (establishing myself in his memory is going to be difficult enough, let alone his regard), I may then set about joining the WRNS providing my salary will be made up to me and my pension rights safeguarded.

To be fair, this represents quite a sacrifice on her part as she will be lonely without me. Or perhaps I should say alone, because I think she is always lonely whether I am with her or not. I wish when we are together we could be a bit more jolly. We had such fun when Daddy was alive, but now she is dedicated to not enjoying herself. If I recount something amusing which has happened during the day, she says, 'That must have been nice, dear,' a shade reproachfully; if it is something rather splendid I have to tell her, she says, 'Yes, I can see you would have enjoyed that,' there being the faintest suggestion of insensitivity on my part. Her face has become so sad, all her features have resigned themselves to unhappiness – in a dignified way, of course; she wouldn't permit any obvious sagging, only a gentle downturning. Sometimes I feel I would like to hug her, but she has never been one for demonstrations of affection and she looks so brittle I am afraid she might fall apart in my embrace. I did say to her once, 'I think Daddy would like us to be happy, don't you?' and she started to cry. So now I just keep toiling away at being happy myself.

It is chastening to reflect that in the first seven months since I left school I have failed to find that freedom I imagined awaited me beyond the school walls. Office work is monotonous, with no bell to announce a welcome change of room and subject. The hours compare unfavourably with the school timetable and the precious time left over at the end of the day is eaten into by long waits on windy station platforms. I have only been to the pictures three times since Christmas and on each occasion I was late for the big film and Joyce Pillinger won't come with me any more.

Yours is a different story. When I read your letters I do wonder whether Miss Tobin might not have been right and that refusing the opportunity to go to university is a decision I shall come to regret. But then I don't think she had in mind early-morning walks across the Fens, every blade of grass clotted with frost, a Red Setter frisking ahead. You don't say much about your companion on these walks, but your joy in his company fairly dances across the pages of your letters. Perhaps I shall meet him when I come for that spring visit to which I so look forward. What will he think of me, I wonder? Is he very clever? I should have heeded Miss Tobin when she said that if I wasn't careful you would leave me behind. Your letters are written with such ease. Mine sound horribly high-flown by contrast. But you have much to write about, whereas my life is so dull. One can't write dullness, can one? It has to be dressed up a bit.

Your penitent friend,
Constance

Ealing
May, 1940

Dearest Sheila,

Your letter took me by surprise. There was I, reliving my two visits, picturing you and your companions eternally wading through flowers on the Backs, or drifting peacefully beneath the willows – and you say you are sad?

Sad for friends, splendid in the vigour of early manhood, minds the sharpest they will ever be, who suddenly pass out of reach. Too much passing for such a young place. And, of course, I can see there will be a problem for those who return from the war to finish their interrupted courses. I've heard it argued that they will be a lot wiser, but you reject this consolation. As I read I can hear the passionate impatience in your voice. Wisdom can't make up for the loss of that young freshness, that openness of mind, the willingness to let the imagination soar. Your feeling is so strong that I experience an odd little pang and I ask myself, is Sheila in love? (Could it be the man with the Red Setter?) When you speak of the adventure of letting go of all the guy ropes and allowing the mind to spin into space, I find myself grieving that no one told me university might offer such an experience; when the matter was under discussion it was represented as a hard slog. Your fear for these young men is that great adventures of the mind may be followed by adventures of a grimmer kind; and with the Germans storming through Norway and now Holland, it does seem a bit dodgy all of a sudden. Whatever may happen to the lads – or is it a lad – you grieve for, university experience will be a disjointed affair, something which has happened at different times to different people and impossible to make a whole out of it.

What of Miles, though, the brilliant one who can't fight, or won't, or is it both? He looked as if his continuing presence would make up for any number of lost others. I found him rather alarming. A spirit of anarchy come to mock the pretension of learning. It was the eyes that disturbed, not missing a thing in spite of having a restricted view thanks to that dark mop of hair. What was it the eyes saw? I wondered. I had the feeling that if we were all to write accounts of the afternoon we had spent together, his version wouldn't bear any relation to what the rest of us wrote. The others, although they disagreed so furiously, picked up cues from one another, but not he. He told me he is a musician. That afternoon he was playing in a different key to the rest of the band. I couldn't make out whether he realised it and enjoyed it, or whether he was quite oblivious of the way he was breaking up the rhythms of conversation, introducing discords, switching from major to minor, and mocking, always mocking. Is he usually like this?

Towards the end of the day it came to me, in one of my intuitive flashes which are the despair of family and friends, that he wasn't aware – no, let's get this particular intuition quite right – he was aware but didn't care about any of us, except you. As soon as I realised that was a possibility everything he said and did made sense because it was all a ploy to claim and hold your attention. I am not unfamiliar with attention-seeking myself; but with me it is an effort to make sure I'm not left out of life's little party. With him, it was more like attempted hypnosis. I do believe he wants you under his spell. You, however, behaved as if you were quite unaware of his machinations. Really unaware? Could he have been the companion who shared frosty walks with you and a dancing Red Setter? Somehow, I think not.

To be continued when we meet in what you call the long vac. and I persist in thinking of as a holiday.

Your impatient friend, eager for the next instalment,

Constance

Ealing
July, 1940

My dear Sheila,

Mummy has written to your parents and although I shall see you on Wednesday, I felt I must write.

John was always so kind and gentle. I remember particularly how he climbed the tree to bring me down when your other brothers just rolled around laughing. And on holiday it was John who rescued you from that bad-tempered old donkey who ran away with you on the beach. I can hardly bear to think of quiet, patient John dying with no one to come to his aid.

Sheila, there is something I want to say and I don't know if I'm going to do it very well. John called on us before he rejoined his regiment and we said all the usual heartening things; Mummy assured him that the Germans would never break through the Maginot Line and I trotted out those stories about the Germans having had to put young, inexperienced soldiers in the front line. He listened politely. He seemed much older than when I last saw him. When we had finished buoying up his spirits, he began to talk about the camping holidays he had in Germany before the war. He told us that some of the people in the little town were members of the German Confessing Church (I think that was the name). They had stood out against Hitler and several of their friends and relatives had disappeared. He said that whatever might happen to him, he would never be as brave as they were because they had to act and think alone while 'I am only a soldier under orders.' It was as if he was telling us that something – and I don't know what, but something to do with life and death – had been resolved between himself and these people. Now, when I think of him, it is sitting in our front room, talking quietly about the Germans who were fighting evil before we ever took up arms. I know that a lot is made about the waste of life in war, but I don't think John would want his death to be thought of in that way.

How can we talk about waste? If there is any waste, we are the ones who will be guilty of it. That's what I wanted to say. I hope you won't think this an awful cheek.

My love and grief,
Constance

Firewatch, County School
November, 1940

My dear Sheila,

Have no fear, things aren't nearly so bad as the rumours you have heard would suggest, although a string of bombs was dropped alongside the Great Western Railway line. Tonight Mummy is staying with your parents, who have insisted she must not be alone on the nights when I have to firewatch. Your mother has had a great influence on Mummy, who has now joined the Women's Voluntary Service. I think she is enjoying herself, but as this is not something she would wish to be observed I am careful not to comment. You ask particularly about your father. I agree he is very quiet and I, too, have noticed that he often sits with a book open on his lap gazing into a corner of the room. But I am sure he and your mother will be all right; they do so much for other people it doesn't leave much space in the day to think about themselves.

Firewatching here seems rather pointless. So far, we have had only one incendiary device, which fell harmlessly on the Technical College playing field and was a great joy to the

Principal, who collects bits and pieces of bombs with all the zeal of an archaeologist for a Roman remain.

The Education Officer is much harassed by his responsibility for the staff. When we had the daylight raids, which most of us thought such fun, he was very perturbed because no one took cover. After much brooding, he came up with a solution which would allow us to go on working while not actually in range of the enemy. For some reason it's considered necessary to have a spotter on the roof of the Technical College, and this lone figure is clearly visible from the front windows of our office. The Education Officer decreed that we should take it in turns to watch the spotter and that when, from his vantage point, he gained early warning of approaching enemy aircraft, he should wave a large white handkerchief whereupon we should take cover. Cover, in this dilapidated building, is a damp cellar with slippery stone steps. You can guess what happened, if not to whom. It was one of the councillors, a pink, ponderous man who doesn't like us very much and had called to apprise us of his latest cause for displeasure, who slipped and broke an ankle. His removal from the cellar occupied the greater part of the morning. The Juvenile Employment Officer, a more robust character than the Education Officer, did his best to convince him that this was one of the hazards of war, but I think he is of the opinion that it is one of the hazards of visiting an inefficient, badly organised office.

Fortunately the office building does not merit a firewatch, so we are on duty at the County School nearby. Our team consists of the Education Officer, three girls and an elderly School Attendance Officer who greets us every morning with the words 'Another bloody dawn'. I think we're constituted thus because the Education Officer thinks we girls too young to be put at risk in any other grouping. I'm assured that some teams regard firewatching as an exercise in licensed debauchery.

And speaking of debauchery. . . . There is a man at the office who deals with transfers to secondary school, a matter of such concern to the general public that it is necessary for him to have a little box of a room all to himself so that he can interview parents in private. This, at any rate, is the theory he has upheld successfully against all efforts to make him share a larger room, thus releasing his cubbyhole for the duplicator – which machine at present stands at the top of the stairs in such a position that very fat people are discouraged from ever visiting staff in the upper regions. On several occcasions when I have taken Mr Randall his tea, I have found him at work on pen and ink drawings. At first, he was quick to put them to one side, but as he came to recognise my footsteps he ceased to make any effort at concealment.

'Your pictures seem to tell a story,' I said to him one day last week.

'I'm glad of that,' he replied, without looking up, 'I'm a book illustrator. These are preliminary sketches.'

'Why do you work here, then?'

'Because, so underrated is the artist, his work doesn't bring in enough money to keep body and soul together, let alone support a wife and child.'

'Is that why we all had to work late last term, helping you to get the transfer notices out to parents?'

'You could say I know my priorities. Does that shock you?'

'I was shocked when I had to work so late.'

He put his pen down and looked at me. He is one of those pale men with straw hair which merges into ashy skin. His face looks grubby as if he becomes easily discouraged while shaving and his body has that sort of looseness which comes of never having tried very hard at anything. He gives the impression that however hard you washed him he would never come up looking clean and fresh. Rumour has it he is going into the RAF. One wonders what they will make of him.

'You must be helped to overcome this tendency to be shocked,' he said. 'Otherwise, with your looks, you are going to have an exhausting time.'

I did not return to his office to collect his cup, but later, when I was washing up, he came behind me and put the cup in the basin. The sink is wedged into a corner of the store room and there isn't space for two people to stand side by side, so I didn't think anything of his standing behind me until he slid his hands beneath my breasts. I would not want to tell this to anyone but you, Sheila. The result quite startled me. My body behaved as though it wasn't part of me. While my mind was saying with admirable coolness, 'Hello, what is this?' my stomach muscles knotted and contracted in the most painful way and my breath came through my lips like steam out of a kettle. Then members of the general public came labouring up the stairs and began to negotiate the duplicator. Mr Randall removed his hands, which had wandered to my stomach to be rewarded with yet more surprising spasms, and departed.

The next day, he discovered some civil defence questionnaires which he had neglected to send to the three grammar schools. He asked the Education Officer if I could accompany him to the schools as I was familiar with the work and could help the school secretaries to complete the questionnaire. He said he had overlooked the forms which had to be returned to Head Office at the end of the week. As there was a lot of trouble over the last lot of forms which Mr Randall had overlooked, the Education Officer agreed to this.

The school secretaries did not need any help from me and we had finished distributing the forms before lunch. Mr Randall said that as he lived nearby and we had plenty of time, perhaps I would like to see some of the books he had illustrated. You know your Constance, Sheila. I was flattered as I think I have an eye for a good drawing; and I have to confess I was curious to see how an artist lives and to meet the artist's wife. If my reading is reliable, artists' wives are a very special breed.

As soon as we got into the house I experienced that sense of having gone deaf which I get when I enter empty buildings. 'When does your wife get home?' I asked. He said she was in Dorset, and pushed me into the sitting-room. He kissed me, bending my head back so hard I thought my neck must snap and getting one of his legs in between mine so that we were all tangled up and it was a wonder I didn't topple over with him on top of me. As we lurched round the room in an ungainly tango he contrived to get my dress unbuttoned and my bra unhooked.

Had he cursed or implored me by name I would not have been so frightened; but he applied himself to his task as if I were not a person but a Christmas parcel he was endeavouring to tear open, some of the goodies already on view. I was surprised by how well-equipped I was to fight. The body has several sharp joints, each of which I used to some purpose. I also discovered that I had at some stage acquired a knowledge of the male anatomy and it was a shrewd placement of the knee joint which eventually brought an end to our engagement. The realisation that I could handle this situation gave me a feeling I can only describe as pure joy. When I had adjusted my clothing and he had recovered his breath, I said that I would like to see the books now.

He said, 'Never mind that. You'll make your way in life without having to use your head.'

By the time we got back to the office my legs had stopped shaking and I felt quite self-possessed, although one of the School Attendance Officers gave me a quizzing as I passed him in the doorway. Later, in the corridor, I overheard this man say to the Juvenile Employment Officer, 'I reckon Blondie there is ripe,' and he made a sucking noise as if messing with a juicy fruit. I was so angry I went straight to the Education Officer and told him I had been in the office for nearly a year and I didn't think I should still be doing the tea; either the other girls could take it in turns with me, or there wouldn't by any tea in future.

The air-raid warning has sounded so I shall have to stop now. Let me know what you think about this. I have a feeling your experiences are much more profound.

Love,
    Constance

Ealing
January, 1941

My dear Sheila,

I'm glad you thought Mummy so much better. When your parents asked us to Christmas lunch I was afraid she might not fit in very well. It's not that she wants to spoil other people's pleasure so much as that she seems to have lost the knack of being a part of it. She did do rather well, didn't she? I think it helps now that she has all these tales to tell about her WVS work.

We didn't have much time to talk and as you didn't reply to my November letter I feel a bit out of touch with your news. I hope you weren't put off by that letter? Or has something made you unhappy? Mummy commented on how thin you had become. 'She used to be sturdy, now she is all bones.'

Dear bony one, I don't mean to pry. If you are unhappy and don't want to talk about it, I shall understand. But don't not write. Tell me the dreary things, or send a postcard saying no news from Cambridge. Anything so long as I know you haven't written me off as too trivial to bother with.

Your loving,
Constance

Firewatch, County School
January, 1941

Dearest Sheila,

How good of you to write at once when you are feeling so wretched. Whatever the trouble, it will pass because you are not the sort to go under for long.

The Randall affair is an episode in the past. Those delicate artist's hands are now sorting screws at an RAF base. He came to the office to show off in uniform. How can I blame him when I shall soon be doing the same thing? I have been accepted for the WRNS and expect my call-up papers any day now. Rejoice with me.

Much love,
Your excited Constance

*Royal Naval Air Station in
the West Country
Time and place: the Control
Tower at dead of night
April, 1941*

My dear Sheila,

I am sorry to have been so neglectful, though I did send postcards, which may have been lost in the bombing. I will try to make amends now, while I wait for the 0100 chart.

Mill Hill Training Centre was splendid. All the girls so attractive and from such distinguished backgrounds – diplomatic corps, Harley Street, the Inns of Court. I visited the home of a girl whose mother was a famous ballerina. They have a basement flat in Holland Park. Mother was elderly and gaunt, wrapped in a rug, only the head, swathed in a turban, visible. She talked about bad plumbing in a husky voice like Garbo's; with a voice like that you don't need subject matter. On our last evening four of us had drinks at the Berkeley. This is it, I thought: life will never be the same again.

After Mill Hill came the course. My category is meteorology. I had been determined to become a coder since they have the best chance of serving abroad. It seems, however, that coding can have a bad effect on people of a nervous disposition and the Wren officer in charge was adamant that I am nervous. She also had doubts as to my stamina and ruled out such categories as radio mechanic, parachute packer and boat's crew. I began to be afraid she would pronounce me generally unfit, so when she suggested that the Met. branch might manage to absorb one highly strung, debilitated Wren, I submitted gratefully. In six weeks I learnt to recognise a surprising number of cloud formations, to assess cloud height and estimate visibility, to read a variety of instruments and to attend to a teleprinter which disgorges sheets of figures which must then be translated into meaningful symbols on a weather chart. Mercifully, the thinking is done by the Met. Officers.

By the end of the course we were all fast friends and we went out to lunch at the Old Chesil Rectory in Winchester. It was all so glorious, the days sped by and only now do I find time to write.

I have been drafted to the West Country. Not to the Doone Valley or the wilder reaches of Exmoor, to the mysterious Somerset Levels or the dancing streams of Dartmoor. This is scrubby, neglected land in which discouraged trees and hedges form random knots, a little patch of earth which no one has ever cherished. Desolation without grandeur. Its one virtue is that it is flat, so the Navy has imposed an airfield upon it, adding its own debris to Nature's scrapyard.

If you can imagine a cross between a caterpillar and a snail, you have a picture of our living quarters. There are some twenty of these molluscs, graced by the homely word 'cabin', each of which accommodates fourteen Wrens. Seven double-decker bunks group around a stove and the place reeks of defeated attempts to get the wretched thing alight. This is Tess of the D'Urbervilles country, sure enough, the crust of civilisation pitifully thin. Woman's lot has not notably improved. Tess might well have preferred the turnip field to labouring from dawn to dusk on an exposed airfield.

This particular airfield has been specially designed to be as uncomfortable as possible for the personnel. The Navy's word for it is 'dispersal', which means that each building is as far away as possible from any other building with which it may share some common purpose. So the ground staff spend a lot of time cycling from one part of the Somerset/Dorset border to another. Naturally, sleeping quarters are dispersed as well, while ablutions are a route march away.

I am in B camp, which is in a small clearing in a wood. When I joined up my mother said, 'At least the Wrens are ladies.' However else one might describe the occupants of cabin 5, lady is not the word that would immediately leap to mind. Long days spent working on the flights have not only toughened, but coarsened, the air mechanics to such an extent that I am told the sailors are deeply shocked by their indelicate language. (Sailors are in some ways as old-fashioned as my mother.) In addition to the air mechanics, we have two messengers from Liverpool who appear to be stitched into their underwear for the duration and a debutante who never washes from the neck down and who dispenses with underwear altogether when she goes out of an evening.

Finally, we have two lesbians. They really do exist outside the covers of *The Well of Loneliness*. The cook stewards, who adopt a very moral attitude to this, have obviously decided that all the occupants of cabin 5 are contaminated and thrust food at us with loathing. When we come back from night duty we find they have forgotten to leave any food out for us. For this reason alone we wish that Jill and Hilda would save their demonstrations of affection for more private places. But they persist in holding hands in the queue in the mess and then sit side by side, Jill's head resting against Hilda's shoulder, while the stewards gaze pop-eyed with wrath, righteous bosoms swelling above the food trays.

I concede that I have been spoilt and closeted, that I am an only child and sensitive to boot. I accept that this experience will do me more good than dining at the Berkeley and that I shall emerge from it a wiser and better person, but the fact remains I find it unpalatable. It wouldn't be so bad if the place were clean, but squalor seems to go hand in hand with dispersal. On a cold morning it is easier to touch up yesterday's face than to squelch down to the ablutions. Cats abound and get into the mess where they have the pick of the food before it gets on to our plates. Discipline is lax because in these conditions it is not easy to find out what is going on, supposing anyone cared.

Saturday is different. On Saturday night a dance is held at A camp. Then the ablutions are crowded and irons are taken from their hiding places. Hair may even be washed. Mirrors are tipped against bunk heads and a new face is created for the coming week.

I went to the ball feeling like Cinderella and had my first success since arriving here. He is a Lieut-Commander, six foot plus and every bit as handsome as Gary Cooper. The officers come late to the dance and stand looking around in a bored fashion to see if there is anything worth their attention. My height is usually against me on such occasions. I was considering taking my leave as I hadn't danced much when he came to me, straight as an arrow, hands outstretched in a gesture which seemed to say that with me in the room what other choice could there be? I have yet to find out whether this is a habit of his; he does have rather an abundance of charm. Whatever the outcome, my stock has undoubtedly gone up with my cabin-mates. Apparently a two and a half ringer is a real catch. He is taking me to dinner in Yeovil tomorrow evening.

This is all a bit rubbishy, isn't it? But you did plead for news.

On a higher plane, I am reading *Howards End* on your recommendation and long to discuss it with you. Did you entirely believe in Howards End itself? It seemed false to me, too idealised, not grounded in the mud of centuries (you will see I am now somewhat of an expert on country living). It left an impression of a rambling country house with a pretty garden, like the pictures on calendars; not authentic enough to make me accept that it stood for abiding things. I thought Tibby was the character who rang most true. There! Now you can come at me.

How exciting it will be if you do manage to get down here in the long vac. As well as arguing about Forster, we might get to the theatre in Salisbury.

The teleprinter is stuttering into action so I must attend to its demands.

    Much love,
        Constance

RNAS
November, 1941

Dearest Sheila,

That lost pastiche of *The Family Reunion* turned up in my gas-mask holder, where I had stuffed my sweet ration and a sanitary towel and where it got horribly mangled. I discovered it as soon as I got back from our Salisbury weekend. It is enclosed with my apologies.

Certain lines touch a chord in me. 'I do not want to go through life alone/Journeying from darkness into darkness/Touching no other traveller on the way.' All is over with the flying instructor; he went the way of Gary Cooper, but not before he had told me that I was a tease, promising more than I was prepared to deliver. The truth is, I have discovered a deep reserve of virtue within myself. Is this unusual or is it more natural in a woman than one is currently led to suppose? It's noticeable that although promiscuity is rife here, only a few girls seem to get genuine pleasure out of it. The rest are eager to protect their reputation against any suggestion of morality. We have established, by some mysterious, unspoken process, that there are four of us in this cabin who are virgins. We view one another thoughtfully from time to time, wondering whether our number has diminished.

And you? You have recovered some of your old sparkle, but I get the impression that although you have found Cambridge intellectually stimulating it hasn't been an entirely happy experience for you. Tell me it isn't your experience you have put into those lines 'Then you have not known what it is to despair;/To knock on a door which will not be opened/To ask for that which cannot be given;/You have never followed a guiding star/Only to discover at the end of the journey/That it was all a mistake and there is no stable.' All doors will open to you. You have so much to give and are prepared to take risks when I would hold back.

I am rereading *The Family Reunion*. How fierce you are! I see what you mean about his characters. It is true that as well as being dreary and self-pitying, Mary doesn't add a thing to the play apart from talking to Harry about their childhood and walking round the table at the end blowing out candles. And the chauffeur is indeed a cross between Bunter and Lob. But I do put in a plea for the poetry. He has such a gift for expressing the kind of uneasiness which lies just beneath the surface of life – 'The attraction of the dark passage, the paw under the door . . .'. Ugh! And what about, 'We do not like to look out of the same window, and see quite a different landscape./We do not like to climb a stair, and find that it takes us down.' There, I feel better now. Nothing like a literary *frisson* to clear away melancholy.

Now to the good news. You remember meeting my one and only friend here, Barbara – she with the mop of flaxen hair and Harpo Marx eyes, whom you found so amusing. She has been drafted to a station not far from Cambridge where she plans to create, by fair means or foul, a vacancy in the Met. Office. It would be nice to see you more often. I have been aware for some time that we begin to speak a different language. But that's to be expected, isn't it, our present ways of life being so different? I'm sure we can still find things to do which we shall both enjoy.

    Much love,
      Constance

RNAS, East Anglia
October, 1942

My dear Sheila,

    Audacious, telling the recruiting officer about school and the part-time Red Cross work and neglecting to mention university. But wise? A first-class degree would probably have ensured you a place among all those brilliant people at that most secret of all establishments, Bletchley, and even if the work proved dull, which it's hard to credit, the company would surely be scintillating. You may think you are sick to death of clever people, but in a short time you will be consumed with a gnawing hunger for intelligent conversation. You will, of course, realise that this reprimand is prompted by pure jealousy. Harpo says I am hopeless on a bicycle and given a small craft to manoeuvre in a crowded harbour I'd be as dangerous as a floating mine. Be that as it may, if there is one category I would prize above all others it is Boat's Crew.

    Guess who I met in Petty Curie the other day? He stepped out of a bookshop, wearing a raincoat several sizes too large and plimsolls with the toes poking through. What impressed me most was his hair, cut short, curls clustered so neatly round his head I quite expected to glimpse Pan's horns peeping out. He suggested we have tea. His face, now the shrubbery has been cut back, is all sharp angles and gleaming planes, not a soft surface anywhere. By contrast, Ronnie, my man of the moment, looks as if he is made of marzipan. I wasn't sure how I was going to manage with your Miles. There are rules of procedure which govern most naval engagements.

I need not have worried since it wasn't me with whom he was concerned. As soon as we had been pushed into a dark corner by a disapproving elderly waitress, he contrived to get me talking about you without himself ever mentioning your name. I'm sure he is not interested in Edith Evans, but he used her as a means of bringing the conversation round to the weekend we spent in Salisbury. Did you tell him about that awful play? I responded by telling him about the two Poles at the dance who accused us of being cold Englishwomen with narrow hips; and I described how you retorted – all scornful pride and flashing eyes – that you came of a Russian *émigré* family and shook them out of their tentative disbelief by spitting at one of them. There was something in the way he listened which suggested he was attending to a dominant theme that ran beneath my piping.

'What sort of music do you write?' I asked.

'How many men have you slept with?' he replied, as if returning one impropriety with another.

I said, 'Sometimes on Mondays and Thursdays; never on early closing day,' and he said, 'Nothing you would recognise as a tune.'

Then, just as I was about to introduce him to Mozart, he said, 'When I first met you, you said it was your ambition to be in the Navy. So why the Fleet Air Arm?' Soon we were talking about the few opportunities open to Wrens to get on terms with His Majesty's ships – for example, boarding officer, boat's crew. . . .

'Sheila is to train as boat's crew,' I said, tiring of this game. 'But then, I expect you knew that.'

He gave me another of his odd, inappropriate looks, glinting and amused, almost triumphant, as though we were playing forfeits and I had been the first to mention a forbidden name.

'And you?' I said. 'We haven't talked about you. What are your plans?'

He blinked his eyes rapidly as if getting rid of a speck of dust. Has it ever occurred to you that he was born with an instant sorting mechanism which deflects all that is not of immediate interest to him so that it doesn't impinge on his consciousness? I swear he blinked me out of his vision. He looked around for a waitress and a skinny waif who couldn't have been in her teens zoomed up as if magnetised. She had consumptive pallor and bruised violet eyes. He must have been in the place before, it certainly wasn't the first time she had feasted those ravenous eyes on him. If she survives she will grow into one of those women with a voracious appetite for self-abasement. Miles, having conjured her up, showed no further interest in her.

I was cross by this time, so I hitched on my shoulder-bag and prepared to take leave of him. 'Shall I give Sheila a message from you?'

He counted out coins with all the reluctance of a thrall forced to pay Danegeld. Then he began to laugh. He looked at me and laughed again, as though I were some comic hiccup in his morning, like a broken flagstone.

When I was half-way down the street, he caught up with me. He might have come through a rainstorm; his face had been washed of all its mischief and wrung out, wrinkled as wash-leather.

'Yes,' he said. 'Tell her you've seen me. Tell her.'

'Tell her what?' He was so urgent, I was taken aback.

'How things are with me.' He was shouting and people turned to stare.

'But I don't know how things are with you,' I protested, feeling exposed and stupid.

'It's obvious, isn't it? You can see, can't you?'

There were tears in his eyes. I lost my temper and shouted, 'But you? How much do you see?' At which he left me.

There is something so odd about him. Surely, most of us learn about life from one another. We observe the passing scene and see how we fit into it, note the behaviour of others and think – so this is the way it works, this is how it's done. Miles, on the other hand, gives the impression that life is something he makes up as he goes along. He is like a giant spider, weaving a web of fantasy round himself. I don't know whether I should have written to you about him.

Yours in perplexity,
        Constance

Ealing
February, 1945

My dear Sheila,

I shall miss you sorely. How lucky we were to have those years together in East Anglia.

Time has flown on this leave. Mummy insists on behaving as if I were being drafted to Ceylon instead of Ireland and many hours have been spent on unnecessary shopping expeditions and the visiting of friends and relatives whom I shall not see again for six months, if ever. She is very distressed. I keep pointing out that even if the Irish do live with their pigs, the Navy won't expect its personnel to go native. But not only does she load me with preventive medicines, she insists on spending her precious coupons on unnecessary comforts. She is undoubtedly confused about climate, but I'm unable to convince her that in all probability it will be warmer in Belfast. Then there is the fact of there being Catholics lurking at every street corner, murdering innocent Protestants when they are not blind drunk on poteen. I don't know which of the Four Horsemen she expects me to encounter first. All of which only fuels my eagerness to explore this country so rich in legend.

You will write often, won't you? It will seem strange at first, with that stretch of sea between me and home.

I shall want to hear about you and Jeffery. The last time we were together you asked whether I was shocked. I'm impressed by how brave you've been, plunging in while I still run up and down the beach, occasionally letting the water lap over my feet but darting back when I feel the pull of the tide. I've noticed when you're with Jeffery that you have a confidence which I lack, a confidence which comes of knowing how much you have to give. Is it that we can't tell what is hidden within us until someone has rifled the store? Oh dear, oh dear. Sometimes as I look at my face in the mirror, putting on my cap at that jaunty angle which so displeases First Officer, I ask myself, is this the only misdemeanour for which I am to be remembered in the Women's Royal Naval Service?

What I said about all Americans being misunderstood husbands wasn't meant to apply to Jeffery. It must be very hard for him, with such an unsympathetic wife yet caring so much for his children. Jeffery has been honest with you, but my American didn't tell me he was married until we had been going out for three months. I admit that at first I was relieved to get the falling in love business over and done with, the authentic pain, humiliation, disillusion, *et al*. It's the sour aftertaste that is hardest to bear. I feel about men as dear Harpo does about lobster, unable to enjoy them because one once did her a mischief.

It's time for new experiences. In Ireland I shall devote myself to myth and legend and make pilgrimages to Dublin and Sligo and Innisfree. I might even learn to play the harp.

I will let you have my address as soon as I arrive.

    Love,
        Constance

Belfast
March, 1945

My dear Sheila,

It was a grey, blustery day when we steamed out of Stranraer and the ship heaved all the way across like a mortally sick animal – we were told it had been used for cattle before the war. I didn't actually throw up, but I felt as if my intestines had been loosened and were slopping about like displaced cargo. Most of the passengers were soldiers. The Army doesn't travel well by sea. I huddled on deck as we came into Larne, wet and cold and no longer very expectant. There it was before me, a low coastline, not spectacular but intensely green even on this grey day. It didn't make much of its fabled charms; it simply rolled out its green mantle like a drapery assistant who knows one will be unable to resist the richness of her cloth. I was in love before I ever landed.

The Met. Wrens are billeted in a small house on the outskirts of the town. From here, we can bicycle into the country in a matter of minutes. Yesterday we hitch-hiked to Cushendun, which is a Catholic village. The man who gave us a lift advised us to get out before dark. One never knows with the Irish whether they are serious or just amusing themselves at one's expense. Certainly, the locals weren't friendly. The woman in the post office would have liked the stamps to be heavier so she could have thrown them at us. It all seems rather comic, but we did get out before dark.

An Irish officer tells me they still celebrate the Battle of the Boyne. The Orangemen swagger through the streets, beating drums and blowing fifes; then in the evening they all get drunk and the Protestants beat up the Catholics. It sounds a bit silly to me. I mean, how long ago was the Battle of the Boyne? I don't think I shall be able to take all this Irish feuding seriously, even though the Catholics do kill an English soldier every now and again to discourage the others.

This seems to be a land haunted by the past. The countryside abounds in ruins – not English ruins, with holes for windows and slates off the roof; whoever ruined these buildings did a thorough job of it, the walls are mostly down to shoulder level. Sometimes one comes across imposing iron gates with nothing beyond to show that a house has ever been there. It tinges the countryside with melancholy. The cottages snuggle so close to the ground that at a distance they seem to be no more than an outcrop of rock.

I have attracted the attention of Number One, a prodigious roué. He is aware my heart has been broken and that in consequence I am very fragile. His intentions appear to be honourable. He is nearly forty and treats me like a daughter. We go to concerts and he tells me no one can enjoy music fully without having experienced the joys of sex. It wounds him to think of how incapacitated I am. I look at all the people listening with glazed expressions and wonder whether they are throbbing with sex. He thinks I am in danger of becoming sentimental about the Irish, whom he regards as bog peasants, and he plans to take me to the West the better to demonstrate his point. I don't think I shall come to any harm with him. A sheep in wolf's clothing.

Let me have your news as soon as you can.

Love,
　　　Constance

Belfast
March, 1945

My darling,

I read your letter in growing astonishment and outrage. He needs time to think? What is this all about? He had an unconscionable long time to think before you gave in to his pleas. How come he didn't discover he was so sensitive then?

I am amazed at your ability to stand back from a situation in which you are so deeply involved and see yourself as only a part of the whole. Were it me, the entire world would be reduced to a tiny globe containing only me and my woe. Yet you see Jeffery with such clarity, undistorted by bitterness. You believe he wants you above all else, but he can't live on the level of his own longings; he is a man who will always run for safety and his tragedy is that he knows it. I don't see Jeffery as the stuff of tragedy. I see him as a bit player who will always miss his entrances and fluff his most important lines.

Just supposing, when he has done his thinking – and always assuming he won't be posted to some unit where he might actually have to fight – he decides he wants to come back. What will you do?

Darling Sheila, the future must hold so much for you. Be not too generous with this craven man.

My love,
Constance

A long way beyond the back of beyond,
Connemara
April, 1945

My dear Sheila,

I'm here, not with the roué as you might have imagined, but with an Irish officer I may have casually mentioned in a previous letter. His name is Fergus Byrne. He is twenty-nine (I winkled that out of the Commander's writer). He is tall and has the sort of frame which looks as if it had left space for future development. His hair is soft and reddish and fluffy and I look at it fondly because I can see it will part company with him some time in his thirties; it's that kind of hair and it is already in retreat. I don't think he will look particularly distinguished bald, but he has a good, nobbly sort of face which will rise above adversity and the eyes won't change – blue and tending to look into the far distance where something amusing seems always to be happening. A generous mouth.

All this on a rather short acquaintance. He asked me to spend this short leave with him at a time when we hardly knew each other. His intentions appear to be honourable. Is it simply that he likes my company? Are we to remain good friends?

We have spent hours trudging across moorland and scrambling over rocks. There have been times, so bumpy is our passage, when physical contact has been made abruptly and I have not found this unpleasing. On the occasions when we have touched, he has seemed to hold me steady as though he were keeping us both on course. For what? I would like to think that this forbearance represents what I am sure Miss Addiscombe would have called respect. He is a Catholic. Do you think Catholics are particularly respectful, or could it be he is indulging in some hitherto undisclosed Irish roguery?

Whatever happens, we have shared experiences I shall always remember. The place where we are staying is out in the country and out in the country in Connemara bears no resemblance to what passes for country in Suffolk or Essex or places south. The fields are littered with rocks and at a distance the landscape is like one gigantic, untended graveyard. Closer inspection reveals that some of the rocks are in fact dwellings. At one such dwelling we stopped, as I thought, for a drink. The woman who served us had red hair which puzzled me, it was so fiery. Red hair fades quickly. Yet I couldn't believe her hair was dyed; it had life still, which was more than could be said for her tired face. It was a shock to realise, studying her while she talked to Fergus, that she was probably still in her thirties. The brew was strong and the afternoon had dwindled before it occurred to me that Fergus was expecting I would consent to pass a night in this place. Oh, they are a cunning folk! The red-haired woman showed me the room with such pride I couldn't have refused it, even though the space was so restricted I could see no way I was going to fit in, save by sleeping with my body inside and my head out of the window. Later, when the woman brought me a basin of cold water, the children crowded into the doorway to look upon this strange creature which had arrived in their midst. We have now been here three days.

The room is on the first floor, but, as the place was built to house dwarfs, when I lean out of the window I am nose to nose with the donkey who is rubbing his head against the wall in an endeavour to kill off a few fleas. Fergus sleeps on the floor somewhere downstairs. He seems quite at home here and long after I have retired I can hear him talking to the man in what passes for a bar. He is talking down there now as I write this by torchlight. He is a great talker – not a chatterer, but a serious, long-distance talker.

Yesterday, strangers came. Not an Irishman with an Englishwoman in tow, but two creatures so rare they might have come from another planet. Americans. I swear the word was carried around the whole of Connemara: people running by day and riding donkeys by night brought the news to the furthest croft.

By morning there were as many people here as if a fair had pitched its tents.

It is a bizarre and, I feel, sad little tale. Imagine. A man and a woman, brother and sister, both in the US Army, have managed to get a few precious days' leave in Ireland. They have come on a quest, seeking their grandfather's home. The only trouble is they do not know exactly where in Connemara grandfather lived. Communication is not easy. I am beginning to realise it is fallacious to think that all the people who speak a version of the English language are thereby enabled to understand one another – particularly when one of the parties has another language up its sleeve. Furthermore, I am not sure how high a place understanding has in the Irish order of priorities.

In the first instance, the man, Dan, made his approach to the wrong person.

They were standing in the lane when Fergus and I met them, looking at the stone-littered hills. By what series of lies and half-truths they had been led this far, we never discovered. Betty was saying, 'I remember Dad telling us it looked good on a fine day but that at other times it was like a stonemason's yard. I didn't expect the fields to be so small, though – like the squares in a piece of patchwork.' Later, they told us they came from Wyoming.

Betty said to us, 'Grandad was such a big man.'

Her brother said, 'We never met Grandad, Betty.'

'But Dad said . . .'

'Dad just naturally made everything sound big.'

It was then that the old woman came round the side of one of the outhouses. When I first met her she struck me as being a creature of unfathomable wiles and nothing which has happened subsequently has caused me to change my mind. Now here she was carrying a bucket, wearing a shawl over her head, shuffling her feet, muttering to herself and generally behaving like a character out of *Riders to the Sea*. I am sure her keening would be the wonder of the Western World. The brother and sister advanced to meet her. She put the bucket down by the outhouse wall and studied them. Americans don't melt naturally into alien landscape. She gave a crow of triumph. 'And will you be from America?'

They were delighted. He began to make introductions, but she interrupted, 'Then I expect you'll be the film folk that are staying down at Spiddal?'

'Film folk?' I said to Fergus.

'Since Flaherty made *Man of Aran* they have been awaiting another film-maker as eagerly as the Second Coming.'

Betty was shocked. 'Oh, no, ma'am. We're from Wyoming.'

Dan said, 'Is it possible I am addressing Mrs Sadie Farrell?'

An obstinate expression came over the old woman's face; this, I have observed, is the expression most natural to her. Dan tried the direct approach, 'Would you be Mrs Sadie Farrell?' A measure of craftiness was added to obstinacy.

Dan said to us, 'I guess these folk don't trust strangers all that much.'

Fergus began, 'I don't think it's that so much as . . .', but Betty was speaking again and Fergus never managed to say what was in his mind, although I think he could well have made his voice heard had he chosen.

'You see, Mrs Farrell, I think we are probably related.' Betty's voice was solemn and a little unsteady. 'My father was James Farrell. He would have been your nephew, perhaps?' Her hopeful pause was answered by an angry glare. Confused, she said, 'Well, cousin, perhaps? We can work out the family tree later, I guess. He emigrated to the States when he was little more than a boy. But then you know all about that. . . . He used to tell so many tales about his home here, particularly about his grandfather.'

The old woman muttered under her breath. Betty said anxiously, 'You are Mrs Farrell, aren't you?'

There was a long pause, then the old woman turned away and emptied out the malodorous contents of the bucket.

Dan said quietly to Betty, 'Father never kept in touch, Betty; it must have been bitter for his folks.'

The old woman picked up the steaming bucket and began to walk away, then turned and looked over her shoulder. She said with a smile which sat ill on her distrusting old face, 'Will you be taking tea, maybe?'

The children and the donkey watched as the two Americans stooped to enter the front room of the shebeen. The red-haired woman came forward with a baby in her arms. She looked tired and hot. The old woman said, 'Will I make the tea?'

Fergus and I remained outside, observing what went on in company with the children and the donkey. Betty walked round the room examining its meagre contents. The red-haired woman had gone into the kitchen to join the old woman; they were talking in what I took to be Gaelic and the red-haired woman sounded cross. The baby was grizzling.

Dan said to Betty, 'I don't think we should hope for too much. We may be related to these folk, but we are still strangers when all is said and done.'

'Yes, I promise I won't force any intimacy on them. It's being here that's important. Dad always meant to return but he left it too late, the way he always did. I feel he would have liked to see us here.'

Dan smiled. 'Yes, I reckon this would have tickled his fancy.'

Beside me, Fergus whispered, 'Oh, it would indeed!' I sensed then that the Irish find laughter in any event which offers itself, their humour bubbles up fresh and impersonal as a wayside spring and every bit as cold.

The door of the inner room had opened and the woman with red hair came out carrying a tray. The old woman followed, carrying the baby. The red-haired woman poured tea. She had become talkative. 'And did you come on the bus as far as Carraroe? Then I expect they will have told you there was a terrible bad accident the other night. It was young Seamus O'Reilly was going down to town with . . .'. The story flowed on while Betty tried awkwardly to hand round the cups and Dan crouched like Atlas holding the world on his shoulders. '. . . and one cow so frightened it put its head right through Mrs O'Leary's front window'. The children laughed from the doorway and she shouted at them to go away. Betty said quickly, 'We should very much like to meet the family.'

The woman seemed surprised but she gave the children incomprehensible instructions and soon their voices could be heard shouting across the field. Men's voices, further away, replied. In a few minutes there were heavy footsteps and an old man and a young man appeared in the yard. The old man was cross and the young one amused. The family talked in Gaelic.

When there was a pause, Betty said how happy she was to be with them and began to introduce herself and her brother, but they took little notice.

'Is it New York you're from?' the young man asked.

'No. We're from Wyoming.'

'Eileen Cleary that was at the post office at Ballymorgan went to Chicago,' the old woman announced. 'She went to Chicago and she worked in the post office there and she wrote to her brother Finn that she sorted a thousand letters a day.'

'And I'm thinking of going to New York myself,' the young man said.

The red-haired woman looked at him sharply and the old woman repeated, 'A thousand letters a day.'

Betty was looking at a faded photograph balanced inconsequentially on a ledge between a jug and a tankard. 'Is this Grandfather?' She pointed to the groom in a wedding group, a mountain of a man glaring fiercely into the camera with a wisp of a girl on his arm.

'Aye, that's himself,' the red-haired woman said sourly. She made the sign of the cross and added, 'God rest his soul.'

'He's a very fine-looking man,' Betty said.

'A terrible noisy place, New York,' the old man said, irritably to the young man. He turned to Dan. 'They tell me New York is a terrible noisy place.'

'It certainly is. We're from . . .'

The young man said, 'I've heard that in Texas . . .'

Betty said, 'Was it here that Grandfather was born?'

The red-haired woman got up and went to the door. 'He was born in the old house, over there.' She pointed to the outhouse.

The children were playing in front of it, hurling stones through the gaping windows. Grass grew out of the thatch and the donkey was nibbling at one corner. The two women walked across the yard and stood in the opening; the door was long gone and the floor was covered with bits of turf and cow dung.

Betty said, 'But it's so small.'

The red-haired woman put up her hand and pushed at the stone around the lintel; dust spilled on to the ground. 'Yes,' she said. 'It's all very small. That's why Kevin wants to go away.'

'My father . . .' Betty began, but the red-haired woman was walking back across the yard. As she and Betty went into the shebeen the young man was talking about California. The baby was crying. The old man was looking through the window at the field where he had been working.

Dan said, 'I think we should go now.'

Betty bent down to the baby and I saw her press a note into the crumpled fist. 'They didn't ask about Dad,' she said softly. 'I waited and not one of them mentioned him. But this is a present from him to you.'

Dan was standing by the door saying to the young man, 'I've never been to San Francisco, but they tell me it's a wonderful place.'

The family lined up and waved as they went away, a plump woman walking as though a little tired and a tall man, arm consolingly round her shoulders. As their figures grew smaller the watchers moved away until there was just one child and the donkey left in the yard. Fergus and I went into the inn. I said to the red-haired woman, 'What did you think those people wanted?'

She clattered the kettle in the hearth. 'I'm sure I've no idea. Perhaps Gran will tell us, since it's her they spoke to.' She put her face close to the old woman's and shouted, 'Or maybe she will not, for she doesn't know herself. Will you never admit that it's deaf you are?'

A look of sly triumph came over the old woman's face. 'They're film people staying down at Spiddal. I didn't tell you because you wouldn't have acted naturally.' She picked up the teapot and shuffled towards the door. 'They'll be back tomorrow with their cameras. You wait and see.'

'You knew that all the time,' I accused Fergus. 'Why didn't you put a stop to it?'

The idea caused him intense surprise. 'Why ever would I do that when they were all enjoying themselves so much?'

'But it wasn't true.' I was never more Miss Addiscombe's pupil than at this moment. 'It was all a terrible mistake.'

This assertion appeared not to impress Fergus. 'What is so important about truth? They will all make their own truth out of it.'

'How can they? They weren't related. And the film company will never come up from Spiddal.'

'There is money in the baby's hand, and Betty and Dan have got a good enough idea how life is in these parts to keep them talking many a day.'

'I shall never understand the Irish.'

This amused him. 'Will you not? And is it so important to understand? Admit you wouldn't have missed it whether you understand it or not.'

I don't know what to make of this man, but as I see that towards the beginning of this letter I have referred to shared experiences I shall always remember, he must have a point.

All through the day people arrived at the shebeen, eager to be in the film. In a few years' time they will have convinced themselves they were in a film. This, it seems to me, is a people to whom a good story is more important than the recounting of facts, with the result that they have become confused between myth and reality.

As you see, I myself am affected by this strange atmosphere. A great conflict is drawing to a close in Europe and here am I totally absorbed in events in Connemara. Please write and put me to shame by recounting your thoughts at this momentous time.

    Your impenitent
      Constance

My dear Sheila,

I am to write to you urgently about this Fergus Byrne and whether it is serious between us.

Very well. I can only say that when he comes into the Met. Office I am immediately aware of my part in a chemical reaction. Rapid changes take place in my body; the heart rate increases, the pulse quickens, blood races through the veins, oxygen is pumped into the brain. All this, while he actually attends to the route forecast he is being given, noting such mundane matters as cloud height and visibility. How it comes about that after bending over me to examine the chart more carefully, he is then able to climb into his kite and avoid contact with the first cloud-covered hill he encounters, I am unable to understand. I suspect there are moments, hours, half-days even, when I am out of his mind. It seems inconceivable, yet when I look at him, when our eyes meet, I cannot be entirely sure that for him the world has ceased to exist. I sometimes think he has our love differently paced, that he is building up more slowly to some more distant consummation.

Does this answer any of your questions?

Love,

Constance

My dear Sheila,

How I relished your poem about victory celebrations in Harwich, contrasting the grandeur of the speeches with the sailors' failure to comport themselves as war heroes. I like the thought that one of us danced the whole night through. As far as I'm concerned, this war has demonstrated my inability to arrive on time, mentally and spiritually as well as physically, to take part in great occasions. There I stand, always on the outside, wick unlighted, while the wise virgins reap the reward of all that hoarding of oil. I believe there was some celebratory fighting in the centre of the town, but I was on watch. I had a generous portion of our messenger's rum ration and ended up with bad thoughts and a headache.

Fergus and I went to see one of those films about occupied France. You know the sort of thing – the café scene with the man playing the fiddle and a message passed, a door opens and closes, a bent figure scurries down cobbled streets in that misty rain which seems always to be falling in the best French films (though this was actually made in America). It set me thinking about how little I have been tested in this war. What can it have been like to have to act on one's own, instead of in the company of other service people, to make one's own decisions instead of obeying orders? And always alone, unsure of the affiliations of neighbours, or how far the loyalty of friends could be expected to stretch, to say nothing of their discretion.

'What,' I asked Fergus, 'would you do if someone knocked on your door one dark night and said, "Help me", and you knew the penalty was death?'

He said this happened all the time in his youth. 'Sometimes we would have a dozen people hidden around the house.'

'I'm serious about this,' I told him. 'I have dreams of standing at the door of my home in Ealing, peering into the darkness of the Common, wondering if I had really heard a tapping on the door. Then a shadow moves and there is a whispered entreaty. I go cold, thinking of Wormwood Scrubs. If it really happened, I don't know how I would answer.'

Fergus tells me I always act first and ask questions afterwards, so I would let them in. I can't be sure of that. I might just as well slam the door and spend the rest of my life asking why I hadn't opened it. I shall never know. People in the occupied countries have been forced to make this kind of decision, ordinary people like Mummy, unused to letting acquaintances across the threshold, let alone strangers bearing problems.

To you, of course, terrible things have happened. You have lost a brother and your parents a son. But I, bar a few upsets, have had a good time, never staying anywhere long enough to

get bored. Heigh-ho, the roving life. People have died scream-
ing with pain in small rooms while I climbed into my bunk full
of self-pity because no one had noticed me at the camp dance.
Something puritan in me says, 'You will pay for this, Constance.'

So much for dark thoughts. You mentioned Miles casually,
tossing him aside in a few well-chosen words. And that, such is
my perverse nature, makes me more interested than if you had
devoted a brisk little paragraph to his reappearance. Perhaps I
react in this way because I know I first mentioned Fergus
casually. No such tricks for you. You toss Miles aside and mean
him to stay tossed. So we will say no more until and if you
mention him again.

In August I shall be due for long leave and hope I shall get to
Harwich to see you and Harpo.

My love,
Constance

Control Tower, night watch
May, 1945

Sheila, my unpredictable friend,

This will have to be very brief because we have a teleprinter fault and I must shortly get the 0100 chart over the
phone from that grudging maiden at Maydown.

I hadn't expected the subject of Miles to come up this quickly.
How have your parents reacted to this whirlwind affair? Have
they, in fact, met him? And have you met his parents? By
comparison Fergus and I are as formal and sedate as characters
out of Jane Austen.

Can it be that there is something about you I haven't noticed
all this time? You are supposed to be the steadfast one, ardent,
yes, but not rash; resolutely in charge of yourself and events. It
is I who am the flibbertigibbet, liable to make ill-advised
decisions on the spur of the moment.

Whatever the answer, tell me you are wildly happy and I will
set myself to being happy for you.

Your loving, if slightly bewildered,
Constance

My dear Sheila Druce,

You said that in spite of your being a married lady, you wanted our correspondence to continue as before, so I am taking you at your word and hope Miles won't object.

I grieve that I shall never know how you looked as you walked up the aisle. It doesn't matter that you weren't in white, it's the face that counts. Did you walk with modestly lowered eyes or gaze eagerly ahead, were you nervous or too radiant for nerves, or did you go forward to meet Miles with grave composure?

Miles doesn't believe in God, you say, only in you, so anywhere he can worship you is acceptable to him. It has the virtue of simplicity. Just now, my conception of the Trinity is not God the Father, God the Son and God the Holy Spirit, but God the Catholic, God the Protestant and God the Holy Spirit off on business elsewhere.

I hope you will like Fergus. Quite apart from his Catholicism, I'm not sure he will measure up to your standards. As I understand it, your love for Miles exploded with all the force of a revelation while you were watching him teasing out a phrase on the piano. Gone was the capricious student always out of step with his contemporaries and in his place, not so much a person as a coil of wire through which energy flowed intermittently; only the wire was sentient and agonisingly aware of the gaps in transmission. You understood – am I right? – that his fractiousness was occasioned by constant pain. Our imperfectibility is something which most of us accept as a condition of being human, but he, it seems, rages against it. Music dances through his brain and when the rhythm falters, the steps stumble and it is as if he were paralysed. The need to impose order on the dancing notes dominates his life. You have found what you need in Miles – a person who uses his energy to the full while others squander their resources on the small change of life.

Things are somewhat different with me. When Fergus and I

went for a walk in the Mournes last week we missed the last bus. I looked at him, as we lazed beside a stream, and I could see energy leaking from every pore. I am afraid he does a lot of squandering.

I look forward to seeing your attic residence in Shepherd's Bush when I come on leave next month.

My love to you both,

Constance

Belfast
August, 1945

My dear Sheila,

It was so good to see you and Miles last week. On previous occasions Miles has seemed a rather forbidding person, so it was a joy to see that hitherto glowering face full of light and mischief. I had no idea he was such a splendid mime – a touch of malice there, perhaps, but who am I to complain of that! And he laughed at himself when he played the piano with mock seriousness; that was unexpected. A quick, dancing wit. You will find him an exhilarating companion. I came away elated.

As I promised, I called on your parents the next day. I know you're troubled about your father and he does indeed seem saddened that you are not making use of your gifts. Your mother said to me, 'He had such hopes for John and now that disappointment has become focused on Sheila.' But I am sure you are wrong in thinking your mother has reservations about Miles. It is just that she fears musicians are not easy to live with. I said, 'She wasn't brought up to want an easy life above all else, was she?' She laughed. It is always possible to tease your dear mother into a good humour. Things will work out well eventually.

Your problems are as nothing compared with those which await me when – and if – I introduce my mother to a Catholic boyfriend. Do you remember Dr Murphy whose surgery was in Elm Avenue? My mother always lowered her voice whenever she referred to him as if the value of our property would go down were it to be widely known there was an Irish Catholic living in the neighbourhood.

I must stop now as I have to go on watch. A good thing, since otherwise I might well bore you with my trepidation. I wish the world were so organised that one could be sure of pleasing everyone.

My love to you and Miles,
Constance

P.S.   I can't believe Winnie has gone, can you? And Attlee such a dreary little man.

The shores of Dublin Bay
November, 1945

My dear Sheila,

Fergus and I are staying here after having spent four days at his home in County Wicklow. It is early morning and I have come down to the sea in the hope of recovering my equilibrium, though I don't know why I should expect to find it since it wasn't here I lost it. Perhaps sharing all that has happened with you will have its usual steadying effect. You must excuse the scribbling-pad paper and the bad writing. It is cold sitting here.

A grey morning. The tide is so far out that a fishing boat on the horizon seems moored in sand. I did not know that a landscape composed of the more sombre colours could so charm the eye. The villages scattered around the bay are dark charcoal blocks. The sand is silver save for little pits and hollows which retain the blue of yesterday's sea. Birds, black and motionless, cluster around a rock. A chunky boat out of Dun Laoghaire sends a plume of smoke in its wake. Today, dawn and low tide have come together. Nothing stirs. There is peace without expectancy.

The rim of the sky is beginning to separate from the sea and now, with such haste the sky blushes pink with effort, a bobbly crochet of burnt rose underlines cumulus clouds, while pools of crimson and turquoise appear in the sand. Around me where

I sit the grass is vibrant green. Across the bay the lighthouse light has become sickly, ill suited to day.

Fergus is not an early riser, so I shall have the dawn watch to myself and I am not sorry. Things have moved quickly. I had always thought of myself as impatient for new experience, but now I have a strong desire for there to be a moratorium on all change for the foreseeable future.

The sky is aquamarine now, bounded with shirred salmon stratus. It seems the moment to tell you that Fergus has asked me to marry him. I feel a surprising reluctance to become Mrs Fergus Byrne when as yet so little is known about Miss Constance Wicks. All my life I have found it necessary to call attention to my existence by contradicting what other people say because it is reassuring to distinguish my own voice in the general babble of sound. It is not that I want to assert that I am me, but rather to demonstrate what I am not. You, on the other hand, have always been so definitely a person you haven't needed to raise your voice. I have noticed that you can listen and be yourself while other people try to incorporate you in their own person. They never succeed.

When Fergus asked me to marry him I said I couldn't possibly marry a Catholic because I didn't intend to have any children, besides which I was attracted to Hinduism, all those laughing, dancing gods. I hadn't, I said, any time for a god who didn't laugh and dance. Fergus listened as though my words were ripples barely disturbing the surface of some great enterprise upon which we were already engaged. Beneath his steadfast gaze lies a secret merriment. I suspect he does not take me as seriously as I take him.

When I had run out of reasons why I couldn't marry him, I found we were engaged to be married in a Catholic church and the children were to be brought up in the Catholic faith. I am to receive instruction, a procedure which I view with foreboding, as does Fergus. 'And speaking of foreboding,' I said. 'What will your parents think of this?'

In my nervousness, I had sketched several mental pictures of Fergus's mother and father to ensure that I wouldn't be caught unawares. She was dark-haired and milky-skinned, with eyes like water that take up the colour of whatever it is they gaze upon; a lovely, impenetrable woman only to be understood by such as Yeats and him she would lead a cruel dance. Or she was one of O'Casey's tenement dwellers, red of hair and raucous, ready to take on all comers and such a talker she would relieve me of any necessity to open my mouth. His father was a plumped-up little man with a face like a brick and blue eyes as round and hard as buttons; his jacket would strain across his chest and the cloth would smell of Murphy's Bar. Then again, he was pointed as a terrier, dark and merry, paying me compliments which made me feel I was being mocked. I had picked out these types as being the ones with which I would find it most difficult to deal. They had one thing in common: they were hostile.

And so to the evening of my arrival and the discovery that Fergus's mother, a one-time red-head, is a strong-boned woman with shrewd, kind eyes and a manner which suggests she is at ease with life and means to stay so, accepting everything that comes her way and finding space for it with the least possible fuss and bother, me included. I can see Fergus in her.

His father is beyond anything I could have imagined. A tall, gaunt man with huge shoulders and sticklike limbs, he resembles a flightless bird. He has a great beak of a nose which is so in the way of his mouth he is constantly in danger of eating it. He it is who has the eyes which take up the colour of whatever they rest upon. In my case, a Protestant. Did I say I feared hostility? There was no hostility, unless one imagines a flightless bird is hostile when it comes upon some delectable crustacean washed up by the tide. That evening he sat watching me like a Red Indian having his first look at a white woman, savouring the torments he will inflict on this strange creature. Torments of a strictly theological nature, you understand.

Did I mentioned we were sitting by candlelight? I think not. I have put people first and now must tell you about the house. James Byrne, Fergus's father, is a farmer. He is also gentry, which means that his long-suffering family lives in the lap of poverty. Fergus tells me that when they were children (six in

45

all) they only had shoes when their father sold a bull. I do not believe this, but I accept that they didn't know comfort as I understand it. The house is large and draughty and every window frame, door and floorboard complains of ill use. Signs of decay there may be, but not all grandeur is departed. There is a lodge at the entrance to the drive and whenever a member of the family arrives an old crone comes out and with difficulty shifts the one-hinged gate. They have cattle and farm-hands, two maids and a cook. What they do not have are electricity, gas, oil (it being in short supply thanks to a war which was none of their making) and a hot-water system. There are a few candles, and a meagre measure of cold water can be coaxed from the taps by kicking the pipes. What warmth there is comes from wood fires which give out more smoke than flame.

These are not the conditions under which my brain functions most adequately. By the time I went to bed that first night I had been unable to cap the joke about the Englishman who asked for the Protestant church and was told 'Them's the papists and them over there's the apists.' I had been bested in discussion on such matters as venal and mortal sin, the potato famine, papal infallibility; I had admitted to labouring under a misconception as to who was immaculately conceived, had confused Thomas with Oliver Cromwell, and revealed to my eternal chagrin that I was unware that the Plough and the Stars was a flag, not O'Casey's attempt at an Irish *Shropshire Lad*. Most dismal of all, I was unable to play bridge – auction or contract.

I went up the stairs to my room by no means assured there is not enough darkness in the whole world to put out the light of one small candle. The leaping shadows which I had always found so entrancing at children's parties were no longer friendly. In an alcove at the turn of the stairs there is a small statue of the Virgin with a nightlight burning beneath it. I never passed it without feeling that some influence was being brought to bear on me. Even now that I have left the house that light still burns in my mind.

The next day there was no time for fanciful notions. People had been invited. Fergus showed me round the farm and when

46

we returned they were there, apprised of the situation, waiting. When I walked into the big sitting-room they looked like people in shock. Certainly they were too shocked to look at me directly, though one or two may have caught a glimpse of my right ear.

At lunch the man on my left talked to his neighbour about bridge and a hunter he had recently bought. The woman on my right told the woman opposite of a visit she had made to a cousin in the North. She was a dumpy little woman who reminded me of my Aunt Ada; the kind of person who spends a lifetime trying never to put a foot out of place, who is distressed if she is called upon to express an opinion on the least controversial of topics if someone else has not broken the ground for her. Yet here she was, placidly describing, as a normal handicap of wartime journeying, how she had travelled on the train concealing a rubber tyre round her waist. 'A bicycle tyre?' I asked. She nodded, the only occasion she acknowledged my presence. Had it been feasible I am sure she would have seen no problem in getting a car tyre past customs in this fashion. So great is my Aunt Ada's respect for law and order that she would not have consented to carry a spoonful of tea across the border, let alone a packet. Later conversation revealed that Fergus's father had driven his car without a licence for the last three months, presumably delaying payment until he has sold a bull.

The party broke up after tea. During all that time not one of the guests had spoken to me. Their behaviour amazed me. One hears of people being ostracised because they are black or Jewish or GIs throwing money around, but I had not imagined it could happen to the English. I had thought that we were acceptable wherever we went.

I began to revise my impressions of Fergus's father. Why had he accepted me? Was he an extraordinarily enlightened Christian or an incredibly perverse Irishman? I have come to the conclusion that he is both. When Fergus and I left he took us to the station. I waved to him as the train moved out and he shouted a quotation from St Peter – I didn't get chapter and verse.

'It will be a great disappointment to him if I convert,' I said to Fergus.

'Not at all; you'll still be English.'

I learnt a lot at Fergus's home. My picture of the Irish came to me mainly through songs, the boys Minstrel and Danny, and *Juno and the Paycock* – 'Blessed Virgin, where were you when me darlin' son was riddled with bullets . . .'. I was unprepared for a people, despite the blarney, totally unsentimental and giving a rather frightening hint that once engaged with them in some harmless bit of chaff there is no point at which they would consider it seemly to withdraw. It is there, in their coldly dancing eyes, the willingness to go the distance and more. I now believe in the Little People; they do not inhabit the mountains and glens, but live in every Irishman. I am going to have quite a time keeping the Little Person in Fergus quiescent. It will be a relief when I get him home to England where, I am glad to say, he intends that we should live, him being an analytical chemist and there not being much in the way of opportunity open to him in Ireland. Bejasus, I'll be speaking the language before I know it.

The dawn is long past. I don't know about equilibrium, but I have found my appetite. I am very cold and my fingers are purple, but I feel better now that I have talked to you.

Write to me when you have time. I know how busy you are, but I long to hear about this new life with all its joys and challenges which will soon confront me.

My love to you and Miles,

Constance

Belfast,
February, 1946

My dear Sheila,

What a difference this new government has made in the feel of the country. Perhaps you are not as aware of it, being a permanent resident, as I was coming over from Ireland. Your parents are delighted and so I expect are you. For myself, I find it hard to take Mr Attlee seriously, he is so insignificant one would pass him in the street without noticing. Aneurin Bevan I could wish more passable. My mother's char says it is what the country needs, but she had expected when she voted Labour that Mr Churchill would still be in charge.

It was so good to see you on that one evening, looking splendidly fit, though I do see what brother Peter meant when he said that having married a musician you were determined to give birth to a double-bass. The two men were a bit edgy, weren't they? Never mind, there will be time later for you to get to know Fergus.

We had a difficult time with my mother. The outcome is that we are to be married in Ireland. I am sad that Mummy will not be there, but it became apparent that a wedding in Ealing would be out of the question – marrying a Catholic is bad enough, flaunting it in the streets of Ealing would be beyond the pale. Then there would be the shame of asking friends to attend and have them make excuses or, worse still, tell her they would stand by her, as though the wedding were taking place at the Old Bailey rather than the Catholic church. She exaggerates, of course. Nevertheless, one of our neighbours, who was brought up in a Welsh valley town, told me that as a child she was threatened that if she so much as crossed the threshold of the Catholic church, the Devil would pop out from behind the altar.

Fergus was astonishingly tolerant of all this; in fact, at times it seemed to me that he was enjoying himself. The strangest thing of all was that he and my mother got on quite well. The skill with which each managed to express the lurid views which have led people to murder one another down the centuries, without actually wounding the other, was remarkable. Looking back on it, I can see that the outcome suited them both. We are to be married in Ireland and Mummy can blame the Irish Sea for her non-attendance. I feel like an amateur singer who has taken part in a musical comedy under the impression that it was Grand Opera.

I look forward to the time not far ahead when we may live so close that all this letter-writing can cease and we can get to know each other again.

Offer up a few good Protestant prayers for me in the days to come. As I do for you and the baby, twins, triplets . . .

>My love to you and Miles,
>>Constance

My dearest Sheila,

Fergus and I are in Dublin on our honeymoon. We send joyful greetings to you and Miles and Lynne and are resolved to manage our great occasions better in future. At least we shall be present for my god-daughter's christening.

You mustn't apologise for the length of your letters and certainly not for their content. I could not hear too much about the coming of Lynne. Babies have never featured much in my life and I tend to confuse them with dolls. My mother says there never was a child so prone to break her dolls; the Christmas ones were lucky if Boxing Day saw them in one piece. The result is that I regard babies as all too breakable. If Lynne doesn't cry at the christening, her godmother can be relied upon to shake with fear when she takes the precious bundle in her arms. A fine pair we shall make!

So, details of every stage of development, please.

I must make this a short letter as we are off to the Abbey Theatre.

>My love to you all,
>>Constance

My dear Sheila,

The reason I did not say very much about the wedding was that it was not in itself memorable.

I don't think I told you about my instruction. It was too depressing to mention, even to you. He was a flinty little

50

Irishman, not a touch of the Playboy about him, and he disliked me from the moment we set eyes on each other. He didn't like women – except mothers and daughters, and them he preferred plaster cast. The upshot was that I became very upset. Fergus took a firm stand and said he was not going to have me dragged weeping into the Catholic Church. So he had to get something called a dispensation while I had to sign away any right to interfere in the upbringing of our children. Even then, much depended on local discretion and there was a time when it seemed that no church in the whole of Ireland would open its doors to us. Eventually, however, permission was given for us to be married in a church in Cork. The service (abridged version) was performed in the sacristy with the bare minimum of words essential to get us properly joined in the eyes of Mother Church; there was no Mass, of course, and no music to gladden the heart. We were allowed two witnesses, Fergus's mother and father. Afterwards, they took us out to a very good dinner.

When I look at the pictures of your wedding, how different it seems, with happy people surrounding the bridal couple and you and Miles gazing rapt in each other. Fergus and I are not yet rapt. The first broken promise, I thought, as the third bottle of wine was opened. To be fair, I suppose by his standards he had sufficient to drink but not too much. My standards are more exacting. Heigh-ho! We had a row on our wedding night and suddenly, just as Fergus's rage was boiling up most awesomely, I saw how funny our situation was. For a few seconds he struggled to hold his fury tight and then it all dissolved in laughter. After that, all went surprisingly well.

I would have liked it otherwise – music, a crowded church and me walking up the aisle, one of the few entitled to wear white at her wedding. But it was not to be and I don't suppose it matters in the sight of God.

We had a marvellous two days in Dublin of which the evening at the Abbey was the most memorable. The play was called *Thy Dear Father*; very passionate stuff with a rebellious son in love with an attractive young woman who wore scarlet and much upset the rigid Catholic family who wanted him to become a priest. What amazed me was the acting. I have been used to actors on stage behaving in a manner I never would – very elegant and sweeping, pointing their lines even when there didn't seem to be much in the way of a point, and definitely keeping me at a distance. These people spoke and behaved as any of us might when we thought there were no outsiders present. No barrier existed between me and them; I was there in that sitting-room with them. Theatre will never be the same again.

Are you happier now? I shall soon be able to demonstrate that all is well. Fergus is already demobilised and we shall be coming home for good in two weeks' time. You and I must have the most tremendous celebration. I thought we might have a bonfire and burn all the letters – or do you think we should wrap them in tissue paper and save them for our children? When I reread, I doubt they will serve as a record of wartime life as there isn't much about the war in them. Once I am settled into domesticity I intend to do some studying, lay it all out before me like a vast jigsaw which, when all the bits are fitted together, will reveal what happened, where, when and why.

Oh, I have so many plans! Fergus and I are going to join the Questors Theatre and I should like to act with them if they'll have me. They are a bit choosy, but, as you know, I used to be considered quite good on stage. Then I mean to join the Overseas League – get a bit of London life and brush up my French at the same time. How would you feel about that? We might do a few theatres as well.

And – a big 'and' this – what about our having a few days together in Norfolk, just the two of us, before we are encumbered with children. Your parents would help with Linnie, I expect, if Miles couldn't manage on his own. We could walk along that pebble beach which stretched into forever, remembering our youth before it's gone quite beyond recall.

Think on these things.

Your excited

Constance

My dear Sheila,

Do you find that during the last few years when we have seen each other so often there is much that doesn't get said while we talk with one ear cocked for controversies from the play area? Now that I have childless hours at my disposal there are thoughts I mean to share with you.

Fergus and I are having a day by the sea. He is wandering along the quayside, talking to the fishermen, while I sit lazily on a rock. The children are in the care of their grandmother.

This gap in our letter writing puts me in mind of that scene change in *The Duchess of Malfi* when a couple of lines suffice to tell the playgoer it is a few years and two children later. If you are tardy returning after the interval, you are never going to get a clear picture of the Duchess's family life. I have an odd feeling of having missed out on something in my own life. When Fergus and I returned from the war I thought endless possibilities stretched before us. What I failed to realise was that one of the possibilities was marriage and children and I had already chosen it – plunged into it, might be a better way of putting it. The water closed over my head with the coming of Dominic. From time to time I surfaced, recognised a few blurred landmarks (such as the privet hedge which bounds our block of flats from the outer world) and submerged again to give birth to Kathleen. Now, here I am with time and space for reflection and nothing upon which to reflect. I seem to have grown into a wife and mother while my mind was occupied with learning to cook, nurture, clean house and children, service husband. It's too late to ask if this is the direction I meant my life to take – I am a quarter of the way down the path already. I watch Fergus's receding figure as he goes off to work leaving me hedged in with the children and I say to myself, 'This is for life.' It's not that I want to change him for anyone else, only that I feel there are a lot of questions that should have been asked before I let myself in for this till death us do part business. People make more enquiries about travel facilities before setting out on two weeks' holiday than I made about a lifetime's journey.

Do you ever have these feelings, you who seem to have plunged fathoms deeper than I? No, of course you don't. Tell me your secret, or give me a clue which will set me off in search of the treasure. Is it that you now have a house while we still belong to that unrooted community of flat-dwellers?

Certainly, the house sets you apart. Some houses look outward to such an extent they are little more than watching-posts, like the jungle tree houses where people crouch to observe the animal life. Nothing goes on inside, it is all happening out there. Other houses close around one tight as a badger's sett. Yours is neither of these. In imagination now I walk down an ordinary suburban street, past semi-detached villas which fill in the spaces between Victorian houses. Flowers and cats look out, a woman sews close up against a window to catch the last of the light. A child's scooter is upturned on a path and further on there is a wheelbarrow full of autumn gold. A man is clipping a hedge and he tells me it is the 'last time this year, with any luck'. A radio is playing in a garage across the road. I come to one of the Victorian houses, standing alone behind a hedge which hasn't come in contact with clippers for a long time. The gate is open because it doesn't close. I walk through undergrowth to a door half hidden by creeper. At my approach the door opens, which is a relief as it doesn't have a knocker and the bell-rope is no longer a part of any ringing system.

As in a fairy story, I step out of the everyday world. I look around the magic place I have entered and realise that the fairy stories are wiser than I had understood. For this is a magic which we could all enjoy, if only we would create our own enchantment.

Time is the first thing to master. It has to be understood that time, in the Druce household, is different from time as most of us know it. I, for example, am the slave of mealtimes. On a Sunday all my energy is devoted to ensuring that the steaming cauldron and the members of my family arrive at the same place at the same time. Whereas in your home, meals wait on the convenience of the inhabitants. And then there is the matter of furnishing. Your rooms are not designed to meet the spatial requirements of sofa, armchairs and table, but those of piano, harp, viola and music stands. When Fergus and I move I shall nag until he has put up shelves. 'If you must have so many books, you should at least be willing to provide accommodation for them.' You, on the other hand, make no problem of this; books are stacked on flat surfaces, mostly the floor, and one thinks nothing of it but simply treads over or around them.

Houses where people aim for conventional standards and fall short are damp with failure. But your house answers a different need – I haven't yet discovered what – and it is joyful. You say that you made a contract with Miles: he could compose and play music at all hours of the day and night, Linnie and Toby (do you only plan to have the two?) could grow up knowing that the rhythm of their life must be woven into their father's periods of creativity, you would breakfast at noon and dine at midnight, with two provisos, first that he did not look for the conventional housewifely comforts, second, that your need to set time aside for poetry should be respected. All very proper to a fairy story where provisos are important and never to be disregarded. I admire you for this. What some people might regard as chaos I see as a great act of creativity, the making of your own individual world. I could never do it, I who am a slave to order.

I love your secret world. Half of my world shuts the front door on me and the children each weekday morning not to return until seven at the earliest, having refreshed himself on the way home. It infuriates me that he isn't rushing home to talk to me. But then I have nothing to talk about except nappies and feeds and feeds and nappies. You inhabit Miles's world. You prove to me that one does not have to open secret panels or travel to distant lands to find enchantment, and although I can't achieve it myself, I feel a need to have some small part in it. And this leads me to my one concern. Is there room in fairyland for people who come and go; or is there a need to protect it from the taint of mortality? In other words, are friends welcome? I did feel that Miles regarded me as an invading force when I came over for the day last month. Dominic was a bit troublesome but, after all, Linnie did hit him quite hard.

Tell me true. Write one letter before we meet and are engulfed by squabbling children.

My love,

Constance

Ealing
October, 1950

Dearest Sheila,

I was delighted to find your letter awaiting me on my return. You tell me that I write better when I'm down to earth. My trouble is I am not content with earth. I really do find in your home an element of magic for which I yearn. However, I take what I imagine to be your point, that I should be making my own kind of magic.

I'm sorry to have called forth an explanation which you hadn't wanted to give. It must be difficult for you, Miles being so possessive, never wanting the neighbours to so much as show a face above the garden fence and resenting your parents' visits. Fergus, on the other hand, never lets the neighbours go until the early hours of the morning if they are rash enough to cross our threshold. Most of them haven't his stamina when it comes to night talk and I watch in alarm as their faces go yellow with fatigue. He isn't a chatterer, make no mistake about that. He likes to get deep into his subject, like a diver moving about in a subterranean world. Your father is one person who can keep him company down there, among weird fronds and reefs beyond which fantastic fish may lurk. He left here at two this very morning. I said to Fergus, 'What did you find to talk about all that time?' He said it was nothing that would interest me.

So we both have problems, though of a different kind. Take heart. Although it must sometimes be claustrophobic, it is not given to many people to be so close to another, so much a part of his being that he draws strength and inspiration as you breathe. There are times when I look at Fergus and think, 'It must be a great disappointment to find yourself married to someone of limited conversation who can't see further than the privet hedge.'

You're still writing poetry, I hope? I would like to have seen evidence of that among the delights of your enchanted house. Recently I came across a poem you sent to me some time ago – the one about Abélard's Héloïse. It pierces my romantic heart and I want it to have fellows. To spur you on, if spur be needed, I'm sending a copy, just in case it has got lost. You're so negligent about your work.

My love,
     Constance

She really lived, Abélard's Héloïse:
From her window saw light quicken on rain-wet roofs,
Leant across the sill to take the racing pulse of the day,
Applauded its tumult
And ran eagerly into the wind-churned street,
The hem of her gown swirling over damp rushes,
The raised hood billowing about a face mercurial
As an April morning.

Or one might come on her in the orchard
Feeding chicken, or standing by a sun-baked wall
Exchanging idle words on subjects of no great moment;
Heedless of the beauty
Which disturbed the senses in that checkered light,
Creature of transient joy, present delight,
The lover of one man not yet become the world's wonder,
Unfettered by legend.

But whether the knot be gently loosed
Or severed with a knife, all loving ends in loss:
Her glory faded, she resigned herself to history
And came to Argenteuil
To wear out the remnants of mortality
In the veiled anonymity of the cloister;

And the nuns who had withdrawn from life before it began
Took her without question

But watched, vicariously excited
As they studied her face for some sign of what it was
That could have inspired so immortal and profane a love;
Raking the dead ashes
For a flame where none could be kindled again
And even the pain of scorched flesh was forgotten:
For them, not less than for us, Abélard's Héloïse
Was long centuries dead.

Ealing
January, 1952

My dear Sheila,

    We still have the plague. Chicken-pox is not to be recommended, so stay away. Another letter would be welcome.

    Love from your wretched and disfigured
      Constance

P.S. How good to have news of Harpo, whom I haven't seen since East Anglia. Miles liked her, you say. I wonder why? How sharp I am become. Men always liked her. She should have married that nice Alan, or was it Andrew? It won't be so easy for her now that the war is over and men more evenly distributed throughout the population. She is one of those women who fail to grab in a time of scarcity. Yes, I should certainly like to see her, but not now. In a week or two, perhaps.

      Constance

Ealing
February, 1952

My dear Sheila,

    The Byrnes are free of chicken-pox and I am pregnant again. My mother puts this desire to have a large family down to the fact that even as a child I always had to be different. 'I knew that when you grew up it would get worse, but I didn't know what form it would take.' Miss Tobin, whom I occasionally meet for coffee in the Broadway, commented, 'You never had sufficient confidence in your intellectual ability.' My poor children, born of exhibitionism out of inferiority complex!

And speaking of inferiority complex, Harpo came. It was nice to see her, but she did little for my self-esteem. She arrived looking more like her namesake than ever, trailing a naval overcoat several sizes too large for her and wearing bell-bottoms. She achieved instant success with Dominic and Kathleen and is already a favourite aunt – and this without resorting to bribery.

She must be very popular in your household, too. Her knowledge of Miles's music puts me to shame. She was so enraptured one felt one had shared her experience. Her lips are permanently parted by those sticking-out front teeth, so it is sensible of her to make a virtue of them and be merry. She looked like the spirit of Christmas goodwill overflowing into bleak February as she spoke of something entitled – can it be? – *Last Thoughts in the Tuileries Gardens*. She told how the violin held the main theme steady on the lawn while the flute and harp sent wisps of regret and longing drifting amid the shrubbery. It was both a salute and a farewell, she sighed, as though briefly the spirit of another age encountered our own and, realising such a meeting could not be, drew apart again. I don't know how Miles would feel about that interpretation? She also said that although it was tender and sad, it was controlled, economic and impartial. I am not sure one can be sad, tender and impartial. Perhaps musically?

I had forgotten that she is a left-winger. But as soon as she started talking about the announcement that we have produced our very own atom bomb I recalled the day when the Duchess of Kent visited the camp. We were encouraged to line the route and do a bit of spontaneous hand-waving and Harpo shouted, 'Vote Labour and lead the freer life! I agree with what she says about the atom bomb – as a small gesture I have not sung the first verse of 'I vow to thee, my country' since Hiroshima – but I blame the Americans, not our way of carrying on at all. I hope that she isn't going to become one of those people who run the country down. It is dispiriting to find that not so long after we fought on the beaches we are villains all. I did a bit of flag-waving and pronounced a valediction on King George VI and all he stood for and then went to bed. Fergus and Harpo talked into the early hours. What did they find to say in all that time? My thoughts aren't of the kind to delay anyone for longer than a few seconds. I see myself wheeling a push-chair through life distributing one-liners as I go.

Perhaps they discussed weaponry. Fergus's lab. has a Ministry of Defence contract, so he is never specific about his work, but I have lately detected signs of waning enthusiasm. In fact, he isn't as enthusiastic a person as he once was. He doesn't feel at home socially among the English. 'What is so special about them that they have to keep buttoned up?' he asks. 'Do they have some race memory of dark deeds which might come tumbling out if they relaxed by their own fireside?' He spends a lot of his spare time working at the Questors Theatre, building sets, which seems to involve considerable consumption of beer. I go along occasionally, but women and children aren't really welcome.

We must meet soon, please.

Love,

Constance

Bognor,
August, 1952

My dear Sheila,

We came here so that the children could play on the sand and all they have done is quarrel. Fergus says we might as well have stayed at home and taken them to the zoo.

One piece of news will interest you. Joyce Pillinger is staying at the Grand and I met her in the coffee lounge on Saturday morning. She works for a film magnate in Wardour Street and if her appearance is anything to go by, it's a very well paid job. She has met Hitchcock and Gary Cooper, whom she calls Coop. She asked after you and when I told her about Toby and Linnie and Miles's music, she made a face and said, 'Yes, but what about her? I thought she was destined to become Poet Laureate.'

She talked a lot about 'our productions' but wasn't much interested in mine. Dominic is always eager to please but he is formidably aware of the rewards that should be forthcoming. I'm never sure whether the awareness of his rights will direct him to the law or the need for a large stage will draw him to the opera. Joyce behaved as if he and Kathleen were invisible. This inevitably led to tantrums. I went fairly rapidly through the advice given in the books on successful mothering. *Ignore* didn't work very well owing to lack of co-operation on the part of the women at the next table. *Explain gently and reason patiently* didn't go down at all well with Kathleen, who resents untypical behaviour in her parent. She emitted howls like rending calico. There was nothing for it but retreat. Joyce was already looking for the nearest escape hatch.

I grappled with my young, watched by the women at the next table. The one with purple hair and blue cheeks who looked as if she had been caught by a late frost, said, 'Of course, it's the mother I blame.' Her companion said, '*And* she's having another. . . .'

As I fought my way past them I said to Dominic, 'When I get you home I shall thrash you within an inch of your life,' which is Fergus's nightly threat to our dog when he runs away on the Common. We left the two women rooting through their hand-bags for coins for the telephone box.

I am writing this on the beach. Fergus has taken Dominic in search of the sea; I suppose it must be somewhere out there. I have never been to a place where the tide goes out so far. Kathleen is knocking down Dominic's sand-castle.

Back to Ealing and that cramped flat on Saturday. I suspect myself of becoming a bit of a misery. Forgive me.

Love,
        Constance

My dear Sheila,

Many thanks for your offer of help, but you mustn't consider coming here with this recital of Miles's music in the offing. Anyway, I don't think there would be room for you as my mother and Aunt Ada feel it their duty to be here much of the time.

Cuillane is meek and quiet and presents fewer challenges than either Dominic or Kathleen. Fergus says this is because she has worked out very quickly how to tell us what she needs. It won't please Dominic if she is brainy. Kathleen is not a jealous child. She seems able to decide what is her due and leave others their share. She has, however, her father's well-developed sense of justice and will fight Dominic ferociously when he indulges his piratical instincts. I am amazed how they differ one from another. As I watch them working at their own personality, dragging it free of the general mêlée, I can see how much I missed as an only child.

Perhaps we can arrange a day out together soon. Somewhere with a lot of space; Richmond Park would do, failing the Sahara Desert.

Prayers, Anglican and Catholic, will be offered for the recital.

My love to you all,
Constance

Sheila, my lifeline,

Yesterday, standing in the kitchen rolling out pastry, the world went out of focus. It was as if I looked down the wrong end of a telescope and saw a great area of darkness and far, far away, something small and recognisable which was the kitchen dresser, minutely neat as in a doll's house. The dresser told me that reality as I had known it a few moments ago was intact. The trouble was that I had become separated from it. I shook from head to foot. Sweat poured from me, ruining the pastry. Had it not been for the children I do not know what might have happened; but as I swung this elephantine head around, gazing down the long tunnel of its trunk, I saw Dominic and Kathleen in the garden, tiny figures about to be drowned in a snowstorm. How many women have been saved by the knowledge that a breakdown is out of the question when there are children to be cared for?

By the time Fergus came home I had learnt to grope about in spite of my disabling trunk. He knew something was wrong. If I didn't say anything about it, his dinner did. He is coming home from work early today; he made some footling excuse, but I know he wants to keep me under observation. He has cancelled his set-building activities for the week. His face has crumpled. I had not realised there is a potential for pain in Fergus. Does he know, has he known longer than I have, that something is wrong with our marriage?

I am become so dull, Sheila. I have no conversation, no interests, not much in the way of thought at all, really. Now, I can barely perform the functions of housewife and mother. I go to bed drained and wake exhausted. Even my kitchen has turned against me, each implement has become a dead weight.

I don't remember what I did at Christmas. The house was full of people. I suppose I fed them.

Help me!
Constance

Ealing
March, 1953

My dear unsympathetic friend,

I really didn't expect a telling off. At the least, soothing words seemed called for; at the best, a personal visit, arms outstretched. Instead, a letter beginning, 'Constance, you silly old thing. . . .'

I was outraged. I continued to be outraged for days. When rage eventually subsided I was surprised to find that I couldn't remember very clearly what all the fuss was about. The situation you described was so exact in every detail I was persuaded I had been aware of it all the time. Fergus loves me, but not Ealing; he needs more space about him. I like entertaining and Fergus likes company. The children are fractious and Dominic behaves like a wild thing whenever he is loosed on the Common. So why are we still cooped up in this flat? It's ridiculous for me to maintain that I need to be near my mother. She has always found close relationships irksome and wouldn't mind in the least if we moved further away.

The remedy for all our ills is in my hands. It's time I provided my family with a home.

I gladly accept your suggestion that Cuillane and I should come to you for a few days next month. Dominic and Kathleen are delighted at the prospect of staying with your parents. Fergus, I suspect, will be more than happy left to his own devices for a few days.

> Blessings on you,
> Constance

Ealing
May, 1953

Sheila, my saviour,

Constance is sane and restored. My days with you did more good than you will ever know.

Rest assured, I found the Druce way of life most agreeable. I have come to realise that I'm not at all averse to disorder in other people's houses – which leads me to the conclusion that it is really work which I don't like. Standards aren't goals to be aimed at, they are crash barriers holding chaos at bay. When I am from home, happy in the knowledge that I shall not be involved in the consequences of their breaching, standards are of no account. I am not one to flinch at the sight of unwashed crockery; dust, unless it makes me sneeze, goes unnoticed; I do not enquire under what conditions the food is cooked; and I regard peeling paint, badly sprung chairs and holes in linoleum as homely signs of occupancy. As for the garden, it seems little short of a miracle that a suburban garden should become a wilderness in which Red Indians may stalk their prey and I confess to a thrill of genuine fear when I was unable to tell from which quarter the attack on the garden shed would come. Dominic and Kathleen would, I am sure, readily exchange the whole of Ealing Common for the Druce savanna.

But when all is said and done, Sheila, there is order in your house, as well you know. Not for you the shrieks and howls of protest which accompany the hours approaching bedtime in Ealing. My heart turns over when I recall those evenings with you: Miles at the piano, you, legs spread beside the harp, Linnie raising the bow to her violin and little Toby fingering his recorder; your faces grave and absorbed, involved in an experience which demands a sharing so complete that all sense of self is lost. This, I would very much like you to know, is my vision of Paradise: a summer evening, windows open on to a garden and music floating into the warm darkness.

Perhaps it has been won at a cost, this closeness that you have as a family. Harpo told me that when she first met you she thought you were going to become so ravishing it might spoil you, the challenging eagerness in your eyes seemed so irresistible that surely nothing could be denied you. You may be pleased to know, however, that far from being spoilt you now have the appearance of having weathered a period of some severity. Harpo sees the need to challenge still strong, but the eagerness replaced by defiance, as though you were no longer so confident that life would fulfil your expectations but intended to go on expecting just the same. Even I, unperceptive as I am, did notice how hard Miles has to work, giving up time to those dough-faced, undistinguished pupils whose parents feel they should have an accomplishment. In my youth, I was such a one. What agony it must be for Miles to have to bear with pupils like me who have cloth ears. If only Fergus could win the Irish sweep, we could buy a house we want instead of one we can afford and Miles wouldn't need to take pupils.

And talking of winning, we now have the result of Fergus's

interview. He is to be the senior chemist – or is it a senior chemist, so proud am I of him I tend to err – in this big new research lab. which was opened recently in Surrey. The pay isn't all that much better but as far as I can gather the work is to do with health rather than defence. He is a happier man and that is what counts.

This weekend we are house-hunting in Surrey and Sussex. Aunt Ada says that we must make sure we have a vegetable garden. My mother says we must enquire about suitable schools for the children. In Dominic's case, I think she has in mind some kind of penal institution.

Have you any orders before we set off?

My love and thanks to you all,

Constance

Sussex
September, 1955

My dear Sheila,

Sussex at last, this strange far-away place from which no 65 bus will take me to your doorstep. I promised to write a long letter as soon as we were settled in, but, as my postcards will have intimated, that process took longer than we anticipated. I so longed to talk to you. I did phone once, but got Miles at what was obviously a very inconvenient moment.

As we unpacked I imagined how those pioneer women must have felt unloading the covered wagon. 'From here on these wheels stop rolling,' I seemed to hear them say. And these are my sentiments. I am definitely a settler.

We didn't have to break virgin soil, but there were times when I thought we might have to construct our own home. You have time on your hands, I trust? Make yourself comfortable, put your feet up. Some of this will not be new to you, but I mean to get this saga down on paper.

Our friends in Ealing said when we finally departed, 'You may have had to wait a long time, but at least you have your very own house.' They, poor things, bought ready-made houses which had all the disadvantages of electric points in the wrong places, intrusive wallpaper and no downstairs loo. We, on the other hand, were about to take possession of a house which represented a series of compromises – between our architect and ourselves and between our architect and the builder. The architect gained the ascendancy over us because he had the expertise, any amendments we suggested being ruled out on the grounds that we were building on chalk; the builder triumphed over the architect because it would have been too expensive to remedy his misreadings of the plans. But people still think we have a house built to our own specification.

If we had had a ready-made house, we should have moved in a year ago, contracts exchanged without fuss; quietly and efficiently we should have set about imposing the Byrne imprint with the aid of furniture, pictures, books and a miscellany of toys. Instead of which we moved in against the advice of our architect, threatening litigation against the advice of our solicitor who, I am sure, has many a cosy chat with our builder at masonic meetings.

I have a feeling, however, that fortune may have changed sides. Our builder has recently been awarded a contract to erect a new estate on a field at the far end of the village. Fergus and I went to see him last week when he was inspecting the site – it is impossible to see him in his office which has a series of escape passages designed to ensure he never comes face to face with one of his customers.

Fergus explained to Mr Buggins (this is not his real name, but I have taken to referring to him in this way in case I should say anything slanderous) that we had one or two things which we wished to talk over with him. While these things were under discussion, I stood beside Fergus, holding my new-born baby in my arms, my other children tugging at my skirts, and contrived to look both defiant and ill used, the way the gypsy women did when they were turned off the campsite near Western Avenue. Dominic, who felt it all very undignified, sulked, Kathleen glowered and Cuillane cried. It would have contributed much had Stephen cried too, but he is a cheerful baby and groped with pudgy fingers in Mr Buggins's direction, his eyes full of delight as if another wonder of the world had revealed itself to him.

Mr Buggins's cohorts withdrew a respectful distance and occupied themselves in an intense scrutiny of an area of grass indistinguishable to the untutored eye from the rest of the field. There was a faint wind stirring washing on the line in the garden of a nearby cottage and I was reminded of the pennants fluttering in that exhilarating battle scene in the film of *Henry V*. I had never before seen Fergus engaged in battle as distinct from argument. He was remarkably calm. If the adrenalin was pumping through his veins, as it was through mine, there was little sign of it. It would not be true to say that his red hair flamed and his face was afire; perhaps there was an added glow of health in his skin and his eyes were shining bright as the Bob Martin's dog; but there was nothing Mr Buggins would recognise as cause for concern.

Mr Buggins is a coarse person and believes that every verb, noun and pronoun should be prefixed by a four-letter word. So cluttered is his speech that it took him some time to deliver himself of even the most direct of injunctions – Get out!

Fergus said he would appreciate it if Mr Buggins would moderate his language in front of me and the children. Mr Buggins said it was Fergus's decision to bring his missus and the bairns along of him. I hadn't realised anyone still said bairns and I don't think Mr Buggins usually does, but some new-found need to win sympathy made him dig into his limited stock of homeliness. He went on to suggest that if Fergus didn't want to shelter behind his family they should conduct their business at some remove and he turned and walked a few paces. Fergus reached him in one stride and spun him round.

I was intrigued. I didn't know how much in control of his temper Fergus was; or whether, even in control, he might not think it a good idea to hit Mr Buggins just for the hell of it. I think the same thought occupied Mr Buggins's mind as they stood nose to chin, Mr Buggins being the shorter. He had the look of a man anxious not to make a wrong assessment. Eventually, he told Fergus that he could get himself into a lot of trouble. He said this with just the faintest hint of sadness on Fergus's account, but as though it were a matter of no consequence to himself.

Mr Buggins's cohorts were edging towards us in a way that suggested they might rally if the standard were raised, but not at too great a risk to themselves. I did a bit of closing in as well and Kathleen suddenly shot forward and punched Mr Buggins on the thigh, thus unwittingly robbing her father of the initiative. Cuillane and the baby cried and Dominic, my first-born, ran away.

Mr Buggins said he wouldn't bring charges against the little girl, but as for her parents. . . . Fergus interrupted to tell him that if he was thinking in terms of charges he should know that there was worse to come. It was our intention to camp out on this site and warn any prospective buyers that Buggins and Company never finished any work they began and, by way of proof, to invite them to inspect our house.

For the first time since I had met him, I felt we had not only Mr Buggins's full attention, but his respect as well. 'It wouldn't do you any good,' he said. But I could see that, good or ill, he believed Fergus would do it.

'It wouldn't do you much good, either,' Fergus pointed out.

'Ay, that's a fact,' Mr Buggins acknowledged without perceptible rancour.

The next day workmen arrived at our house. They seem intent on working hard and appear to bear us no grudge.

Do you ever get the feeling that there is a continuing process of change going on inside you? Consider this affray in the field. I, who had been brought up to believe it was ill-bred even to mention money, not only stood by while Fergus and Mr Buggins disputed, for the enlightenment of any villagers within a mile's radius, amounts paid and owing, but interposed with a recital of figures relating to the heating system. Even more to be deprecated than the mention of money, was the discussion of anything pertaining to one's health. Only the lower classes, my mother had assured me, make health a subject of conversation.

Yet I was prepared to let Mr Buggins know that I attributed to his negligence Dominic's constipation, Cuillane's rash and Kathleen's indigestion. I had never imagined that I would consent to discuss my business publicly or to draw attention to my misfortunes with such abandon.

This is not, I can see, the best possible introduction to one's neighbours. But they, too, know what it is to be out of favour. As you'll remember, we live in a road which has been cut into downland – ours is the last house, the final desecration. Our next-door neighbour is an amiable civil servant who told us things were very sticky when he and his wife came to live here six years ago. 'One can't blame them,' he said philosophically, gazing at his down-scaped garden. 'We ruined the village. Much worse things have happened here since, but this road started it.'

It marks the end of real rural life in Sussex. First of all, they ploughed up the Downs during the war and now that the war is over, we have come. It's all very sad, but I think we will be able to live with our consciences and I expect we will soon be thinking of it as our village and fighting to keep it free of undesirable invaders.

Fergus and the children love it because they can be up on the Downs within minutes of leaving the house – and bring down-land back into it on their return. They are up there as I write.

The people are a mixed bag – a brigadier, an ex-district commissioner of the benevolent Sanders of the River variety, civil servants, a publisher, teachers, and the farming community who stand aloof, one hand on shot-gun, waiting to pick off anyone who strays from a footpath. The people we have so far met socially don't dress up and they entertain modestly. Better still, they drink only moderately but number a few immoderate talkers to keep Fergus company of nights. They have looked us over and I think they have decided they will be able to absorb the Byrnes without too much difficulty once this trouble with the builder is settled. The Brigadier, in fact, approves of Fergus's stand. 'Audacity,' he said to me over his beech hedge. 'Don't see enough of it nowadays. I look at the painting by Goya of the Iron Duke and I see it in the eyes – audacity.' I told Fergus the bit about audacity without bringing Wellington into it. There will be a time for him to discuss the Iron Duke with the Brigadier.

By half-term all should be more or less orderly and we shall be ready to receive guests. Would Linnie like to come to us for half-term? I know how shy she is and I don't want to press the invitation if it is going to be upsetting for her; but you did ask me to be godmother, so I feel I should be allowed a certain licence. It does seem to me that now she is nine she should be getting out more among other children. She touches my heart, she is so meek and demure, like Fanny in *Mansfield Park*. But there won't be any Edmund for her in this age, will there? Not that I would really wish Edmund on any girl. We would love to have her. Indeed, come Christmas, we would love to have all the Druces, if you could ever contemplate such an upheaval. Think on it.

My love as ever,
Constance

Sussex
November, 1955

My dear Sheila,

I was so glad you persuaded Miles to let Linnie come. I can understand his being reluctant to share his treasure. The first time Kathleen stayed the night with a friend there was an icy hole inside me as the family gathered in the evening and she not among them. Then, when she returned, I was sneakingly pleased she was so taken aback because things were ordered differently in her friend's home, neatness taking priority over comfort. 'I didn't know where it was all right to sit,' she wailed. Of course, I defended the right of each family to order its home life according to its own values and I dealt with each specific complaint with commendable charity, but I was gloating inwardly. Yet I knew a warning had been sounded. One day she will go away and find things to her liking which we don't have to

71

give, either because we can't afford them or because we don't have it in ourselves to supply those particular needs.

I had no idea Miles's childhood was so lonely and unhappy, but that shouldn't mean he has to build a containing wall around you and the children. He is under no threat. One has only to look at you to know that you are all brimming with love for him.

Linnie showed us the pictures taken at the recent concert. Miles looked incredibly slim and the tousled hair is a very effective frame for that sharply chiselled face. I said to Fergus, 'See how well Miles has kept his figure, not an ounce of superfluous flesh on him!' Alas, Fergus's appetites are stronger than his vanity and he merely said that you don't feed Miles properly. 'The poor man looks harrowed.' Perhaps you had better not show Miles this letter. In fact, I am never quite sure whether he reads any of my letters. I do show yours to Fergus from time to time. I hope you don't mind? He appreciates your sense of humour and he thinks you can be outrageous in your opinions, something by which he sets great store.

I must attend to Stephen now. He has been left in Dominic's charge and this is a situation which needs frequent monitoring. Stephen is a serene baby, utterly sure he is lovable, but Dominic's mind is full of bad thoughts and I sometimes catch him looking at my angel with pure hatred.

My love to you all and particularly to our enchanting little guest, Linnie.

Constance

Sussex
December, 1955

Sheila!

You lock away my letters. What is this? You need a part of your life that is your own, a place where people only enter by invitation? Does Miles understand this? If Fergus started to lock away his letters it would arouse my deepest suspicions. No doubt you know best, but I am a bit disturbed. I had always imagined you would drain yourself for your loved ones. Far from withholding letters, Miles would only need to look wistful and you would shower them upon him.

One is forever having to reassess situations. I sometimes wonder how much I know about my own marriage. Fergus and I went out to dinner last night. A young woman in the village came to look after the children. 'I think I may have forgotten how to behave in adult company,' I said to Fergus as we strolled down the road, just the two of us, no one lagging behind or running too far ahead, no one wanting to be carried or do a wee-wee.

We were separated as soon as we arrived and for a few minutes I suffered all the agonies of childhood parties where I always seemed to arrive when everyone else was warmed up and didn't know how to fan my little flame. As usual, in such circumstances, I talked too much about too little.

At dinner, Fergus and the Brigadier got into an argument about this trouble which is building up in the Middle East. Personally, I think Nasser needs to be put in his place and that was the Brigadier's view. I had hoped we wouldn't get on to any contentious subjects because I want us to make friends here. Men, however, seem able to disagree without inflicting lasting wounds on one another. I said to the Brigadier when we were drinking coffee in the sitting-room, 'I'm afraid my husband tends to express himself rather strongly,' and he said, 'Let's say that most Irishmen enjoy a fight' and I saw to my relief that he liked Fergus. He is one of those quiet Englishmen, humorous, steadfast, of the type to whom my mother would have liked to see me wedded. I wonder what my life would have been with someone like him.

Later in the evening, looking round the room, I saw my neighbours in the comfortable glow of firelight, good, reliable Anglo-Saxon folk, settlers, pillars of the community, the kind of people who serve on committees, clear the snow outside their frontage and warn the neighbours when they are going to light a bonfire. And then I looked at Fergus. It's not that his conversation is more interesting (only more extended), nor, I must concede, is it his looks which set him apart; it is a quality of relaxation in him, a freedom from a kind of pressure which English people put on themselves. I sometimes feel he is still here on a visit, free to leave and continue his travels whenever the impulse takes him. Although as yet he has shown no footloose tendency, he is not naturally a settler, he has put down no roots in our culture. I shall never understand him. He is a continent of which I have explored only an outer island. So who am I to comment on what goes on between you and Miles? Forgive me.

My love,
Constance

Sussex
June, 1956

My dear Sheila,

Just when we are safest, there's a sunset touch. . . . A poetic way of saying that when at last you feel settled that's the time the unexpected guest will call. For me, to be settled represents proof of good living, a state to which I constantly aspire. Lately, a dreadful doubt has formed in my mind. Can it be that settled is not the natural state of the world?

That was a marvellous letter from you. Yes, yes and yes, I am fascinated by this suspicion of a thaw taking place behind the Iron Curtain. I, too, had thought of these countries as merged into one uniform greyness, sterilised beyond hope, their people reduced to automatons. Now that something is stirring, I find myself painfully moved by this cracking of the ice, the slow coming to life. But you didn't sit and agonise, you went off to the Red Cross with bundles of clothes for Poland with which you could ill afford to part.

It is a beautiful spring day and as I write I can see Fergus in the garden shed. He is supposed to be cleaning his implements. He sits in the doorway, a far-away look in his eyes, completely happy. I never knew anyone who could be so fulfilled by the thought of work. Soon, he will begin to paint the handles, some red, some green; time will pass while the paint dries, June will turn into July and then he will rub the steel until it shines like plated silver. This is becoming a yearly ritual which he lovingly performs while the weeds grow waist high. Some of these implements, I suspect, have never actually touched earth.

Fergus is happy. His wife is not. Cuillane is attending the little nursery school here, so there is only Stephen at home during the day. I have made friends with a young woman in this road who has two children. She looks after Stephen for me sometimes and in return I look after her two. This means I suddenly find myself able to get out on my own. I feel as if I am emerging after a long spell in detention, exposed and unsure of myself. Something seems to have happened to the world while I haven't had my eye on it.

Not only is there this stirring in Europe, but there is unrest of a different kind nearer home. My vicar, an admirer of the late Bishop Barnes, likes to think of himself as a humanist Christian. I think of him as an agnostic Christian. He is young, of a fresh complexion and assured countenance, with thick brown hair *en brosse* and eyes, greatly magnified by horn-rimmed glasses, gleaming with intelligence. It is apparent, as he radiates down on us little people from the pulpit, that he regards the Mysteries – the Virgin Birth, the Divinity of Christ, the Resurrection – as little more than aids for the weaker brethren. I'm not sure where God stands in all this. A mixed marriage tends to tone up the spiritual muscle of the partners. God has become important to me and I don't like to be left behind when it comes to faithfulness. So I made an appointment to discuss the matter with the Vicar.

Let me try to recreate the scene for you. I need to share it with someone and the affairs of my church are not of interest to my family.

His wife opened the door to me. She's an agnostic proper and only married him on the understanding that she would not be expected to involve herself in parish affairs. Unfortunately for her, the parish tends to intrude in the form of people like me.

He seemed to have wearied since I last saw him and I got the impression that he was as apprehensive about this interview as I was. He said, 'I'm sorry if my references to Bishop Barnes upset you . . .'

'I don't mind about Bishop Barnes, or Bonhoeffer, or any of the other people you mentioned,' I said. 'But I do need to know what the Church thinks.'

Perhaps he had hoped that an apology on behalf of Bishop Barnes would set matters right. He blinked rapidly and said, 'Now, what do you mean by the Church?' I have always suspected that people ask this sort of question to lay bare the confusion of my thoughts. I could see, however, that he was giving himself time.

'The Anglican Communion,' I said. 'What is its doctrine?'

'Mmh . . . Well . . . I think we have moved some way from too close a concern with doctrine.'

'Does that mean we don't have any?'

Although in the pulpit he is remarkably free with his ideas, privately he seemed shy about expressing himself. He looked away from me while he answered, like a virgin required to strip. 'The Church is evolving all the time. It is important we don't regard it as a static thing. I like to think of it as the ark of the covenant, which the faithful carry with them on their journey.'

This isn't the way I think of the Church, but if it helped him I was prepared to go along with it. 'Does it have any furniture?' I asked.

He winced.

It seemed that I must do the talking, which was fair enough, since it was I who had the problem. 'What about the Creed? We say it at each Eucharist, so I suppose it must be important, even if it is not the sum of things.'

'It is supposed to summarise our beliefs,' he said irritably. 'It depends on what we mean by the beliefs we assert.'

'Could we go through them? I believe in God the Father Almighty, Maker of heaven and earth. Are we still all right with that?'

He clenched his hands and examined the knuckles. 'How do you think of God?'

'God the Father Almighty, Maker of heaven and earth . . .'

'You wouldn't be happier with the idea of Him as the source of all being, the energy which powers the universe . . .'

'I wouldn't be happy leaving out God the Father.'

'Why do you think the father image is so important to you?'

'It was important to Jesus.' It's surprising the difficulty one has with mentioning the founder of the faith. I felt naive and foolish and I could see he was embarrassed. Perhaps it's not God we need to find another image for, but Jesus. He eyed me anxiously, like a surgeon faced with a patient whose illness is so extreme there is no kind way of tackling it. 'Jesus walked this earth a long time ago,' he said. 'He seems to have lived in a brilliantly lit landscape; there is an electric charge in everything He does. One feels that God is an intense and immediate reality to Him. Most of us can't feel like that. We have lost the sense of immediacy.'

'So that means Jesus has to be altered, not us?'

'Our conception of Him . . .'

'Do you believe in the Virgin Birth?' I asked while we were on the subject of conception.

He thought for a moment, perhaps wondering whether to ask what I meant by Virgin Birth, and then decided to take his stand squarely beside Bishop Barnes. 'No.'

'Or that He was divine?'

He passed a hand across his chin. 'I think God was truly in Him . . . blindingly so.'

'What about the Holy Spirit?' We might as well polish off the Trinity.

'How much do you yourself believe?' he asked gently. 'I mean, do you ever think about these things which you repeat so often? Are there any questions you ask?' He might have been a psychologist inviting me to examine the darker reaches of my mind.

'Of course I don't believe everything,' I said. 'For one thing, my mind isn't capable of stretching that far. I believe some things some of the time and others most of the time. In my black moments I don't believe anything at all. The Virgin Birth gives me a lot of trouble, but I have hopes that if I leave it around in my mind something will grow out of it. But I don't expect the Church to haver like that. The Church doesn't have feelings, does it? It doesn't have off-days, though it does seem to have off-centuries.'

'What do you think the Church is?'

'I like to think of it as a framework, something within which I can move around, test my beliefs, measure my ideas up against its doctrines. I like to think of it as something which holds me; I don't like the structure to wobble every time a bishop has an idea.'

'How would you feel about the Church as a lot of individuals doing much the same sort of thing as yourself?'

'Not good.'

'Would you not agree that God is revealing Himself to His people all the time?'

'But there's a lot of people and a lot of time has passed. There must be some way of quantifying and qualifying. How does one decide what is revelation if there isn't any machinery for examining all the claims made?'

'You don't think that this is something we each have to do within ourselves?'

'Doesn't that mean we end up with one person believing one thing and another something else, according to their make-up and predilections?'

'I'm afraid our "make-up", as you put it, does tend to influence our way of believing.'

'That whittles it all down to something so personal and idiosyncratic that there is no place for a community of faith.'

He spread out his hands, palms upwards. 'If that is how you see it.'

I was beginning to understand how Peter must have felt when he tried to walk on the water. I said, 'I could no more work out on my own how this village should be run, let alone the county or the country. I need to be a citizen. In the same way, I need to be a member of a community of faith; I couldn't exist as an

78

isolated individual, trying to work everything out myself. And I couldn't believe in a God whom I could work out.'

'I concede that. My approach may seem to you to be negative; but I think we are going through a time – a rather exciting time – when great changes are taking place in our understanding of . . . well, let's say God, since that is obviously the term with which you are most comfortable.'

'What term are you most comfortable with?'

'If I could put it into words, it wouldn't be what I meant.'

'If it's as complicated as that, then Christianity isn't really for most people, is it? I mean, ordinary people like me.'

His glasses misted up; he took them off and rubbed at them with his handkerchief. His face looked undefended without them. I wondered if he might have been better off as a Buddhist, then no one would insist he define the undefinable. But I didn't say that. I was aware of pain in him, deeper than any I could inflict and it occurred to me that his explorations are made at some cost to himself. Why people talk about the consolations of religion, I can't imagine.

The rest of my family is safely gathered into the Catholic fold. Dominic, Kathleen and Cuillane are out at some youth jamboree organised by the Church this afternoon. I begin to feel like a solitary sheep left on the mountainside without any tender shepherd to care about its plight.

There! Do you regret that you once said you were more interested in hearing about the state of my soul than what we are growing in the vegetable garden?

We go to Devon at the end of next month, complete with tent – an enterprise I view with considerable misgivings. It seems years since you had a holiday. Why don't you all come here and look after the house while we are away?

My love to you all,
            Constance

P.S.   Isn't it a blight that this pestilential Nasser has become President of Egypt? No wonder I am disturbed.

My dear Sheila,

In haste, as I have to collect Cuillane from a friend's house. Did you know you were in the *Observer* – a picture of the Druces and Harpo among a small group of people attending a meeting in Westminster at which Fenner Brockway held forth about the need for nuclear disarmament? I saw it at a coffee morning in aid of the church roof, but didn't like to ask for it as our hostess was telling all present that Fenner Brockway is engaged in a plot to overthrow democracy. Miles looks every bit as angry as this chap in the play everyone is talking about; Harpo shines forth like Mother Courage converted to peace; you have your head bent, keeping your thoughts to yourself, wise woman. Try to get hold of a copy.

What times we live in! Unrest in Hungary now.

Love,

Constance

Sussex
November, 1956

My dear Sheila,

I am hunched in bed writing this. We have Fergus's Jesuit friend staying with us and they are downstairs debating a book by A. J. Ayer which has just come out. How I wish we two could be talking now. You, at least, might explain with some patience what is happening to our country.

Fergus has always known how perfidious are the English. We quarrelled last Sunday morning. I don't know quite what started it – a news bulletin probably, or it may have been the sight of him up early to go to Mass and all those comfortable certainties from which I am shut out. I found myself telling him that the Irish are always grieving over a country they never live in. When did they ever produce anything other than grievances? What leaders have they ever had – not Cuchulain and Conchubar, but real men like Robert the Bruce and Wallace? Even the Welsh had Glendower. What is this lost greatness the harp at Tara sang? 'It's all in the imagination,' I said, following my little flock into the hall where they picked up their missals. 'It's the land that never was.'

'What's wrong with Ma?' Kathleen asked Fergus.

'Anthony Eden has upset her,' he replied, shepherding them down the garden path.

We went out to dinner on Tuesday. We get invited out twice a year at the most, why did it have to be now? Mine host, a mild little bookseller, was wearing his tank corps tie – remember? brown, red and green, through mud and blood to the cemetery beyond.

'Teach the wogs a lesson once and for all,' he boomed. 'As for Gaitskell, he should be in prison. A lot.of decent fellows in the Labour Party are ashamed of him.'

Mr Gaitskell has been my rock over the last few days and I felt I had to speak for him. As you know, I have no difficulty in being devil's advocate, but when I try to uphold the cause of right the words don't come so readily. 'He is the only person who has spoken for me, so perhaps I should be in prison, too.' The walls of my throat were shaking so much my voice sounded strangled.

The woman next to me thought I was in need of rescue. 'You are like me, my dear. I hate the thought of our bombing the Egyptians.'

Our host said, 'We didn't bomb the Egyptians. We bombed their airfield.'

Fergus was at the far end of the table, talking peaceably about Jo Grimond and the Liberal Party.

The woman next to me said, 'I know we had to do it. I just don't like to think of it.'

Our host went on talking about the Canal, how important it is to the peace of the world that it should remain open, and how primitive people like the Egyptians couldn't possibly maintain or manage it. I sat there, the victim of a ludicrous piece of miscasting. I am not a rebel, a radical, left-wing. From time to time I may have made fun of patriotism, but I didn't expect to be taken seriously. I believe in my country. We have integrity, we are people of our word, and for that I respect us. We stood against tyranny when the rest of Europe had gone under and for that I shall be eternally proud. Emphatically, we are not the sort of people who make dubious secret treaties, attack without going through the proper preliminaries, lie to our allies and to one another. Above all, we do not commit an act of war without allowing our people to have any say in the matter. This is not us. We, collectively, have gone mad. I am sane. Sane and unchanged, not a rebel, a radical or left-wing.

What will my children make of England when they grow up? Will it seem a very different place from the land of my youth? Do they already see it differently because they are Catholic? I begin to feel afraid that they will grow away from me.

Tell me what you think.

My love,

Constance

Sussex
November, 1956

My dear Sheila,

I agree with much that you say but it doesn't make me any happier. Harpo seems quite delighted we have fallen flat on our face over this Canal business; it is as though it had happened to another person whom she disliked and from whom she has no difficulty in distancing herself. But I don't see it like that. It has happened to my country, of which I am a part, not a disinterested observer. England is my larger family. I see now how precious was the sense of belonging within that family. This is the first time I have felt so completely at odds with the people around me and yet I still feel closer to them than to Harpo. I want to think like them, I want to believe what they believe; they are good people whose opinions I usually respect. I cannot understand why I am so shaken while they remain staunch.

It isn't only the Suez affair on which we are divided. It is Hungary as well. My nice bookseller, the Brigadier, even the easy-going civil servant next door, all resent the Hungarians. Not too many years ago these men risked their lives in the desert and in Italy in a fight for freedom. On a domestic level, they are the kind who would rush into the street on hearing a cry for help. Yet their response to that terrible cry from Imre Nagy as the Russian tanks moved in, 'Help us!' was embarrassed irritation which quickly turned to resentment. My daily help produced a newspaper cutting reporting how the refugees grumbled about their treatment. 'All this fuss about these people,' she said, 'and this is how they repay kindness.' As if they were down-and-outs complaining about a soup kitchen.

I said to Fergus, 'We should be dancing for joy that tyranny has been challenged.' He said that people don't like the idea of authority, of whatever kind, breaking down; the status quo, vile as it may be, is preferred to the unknown. Can that be the answer? Or is it guilt? While the Hungarians were fighting for freedom, as we fought on the beaches of Dunkirk, we turned our back on them and got on with our Suez adventure. What would be the use of our making a fuss about the invasion of Hungary by the Russians when we have so compromised ourselves?

I am daily unlearning my country. Do you feel the same? And does it distress you? You didn't sound distressed in your letter so much as very sure and angry. I seem to have the worst of all possible worlds, deploring what Harpo calls the immorality of Suez without being rewarded by any sense of righteousness. I am, after all, a part of that immorality, since I am English.

Fergus has taken the children for a walk because he thinks I am not well. I can hear them coming down the road, so I must pull myself together and reward them with tea.

I am sorry this is such a dreary letter. Perhaps I shall be better when the baby comes.

Your outcast
        Constance

Sheila,

No, not offended. Discouraged. It takes me time to think things out while you seem always to be ahead of me, crisp and decisive. It is rather desponding to have one's loved ones all so knowing at a time when one feels so soggy. When the baby comes fuzzy old head will clear and words will dance across the page again.

Must attend to Christmas preparations. Do Buddhists have a festive season anything approaching ours? If not, I may become one.

Love,
    Constance

My dear Sheila,

I'm sorry not to have written sooner. Fergus wrote to thank you for the presents because I have been unwell. My mother came to help, but it wasn't a great success. She doesn't really like children and certainly not in duplicate. Almost her first words on arrival were 'We don't have a history of twins in our family', as if they were a nasty disease Fergus had transmitted to me. It was like having an exacting guest, constantly demanding what she should do and bemoaning the fact that she was in the way. She meant well, but I haven't the energy to construct a work programme for someone else and she seemed unable to do even the smallest thing on her own initiative.

Last night I dreamt I was in a room full of small cloven-hoofed creatures while in the street below someone had loosed a huge, unwieldy pig. A great boar? Whether I am bored with kids, or a bore about kids, or both, was not resolved. I woke feeling as if I had been a long time corked in a bottle with watery greyness all around.

I hope you can read this, my writing skills have gone along with my energy.

    Love,

        Constance

Sussex
April, 1957

My dearest Sheila,

    The moment you came through the door you raised us all up. You know you have this gift? I think it is so important we should know our gifts, particularly as we get older and a bit more worn, no longer the bright, shining things we once were. You took upon yourself our burden. Were you daunted when you felt the weight? You did not show it. You looked at us, held out your arms and laughed as if with joy. In parting, you have left your gift behind, laughter lodged in nooks and crannies of the house. It is going to come as quite a shock to poor Gillian and James, the discovery that it is I who am their mother. Up until now they have probably thought of me as the wet nurse.

    Stephen seemed to think you lived here. When you left he thought you were playing hide-and-seek and he peered behind chairs and under tables, shouting 'Auntie Shee'. Fergus explained that you had gone back to your own home and as Stephen was not convinced of the necessity for this, he painted a heart-rending picture of Linnie and Toby deprived of their Mummy.

    Stephen has consented to be comforted and seems disposed to be content with his parents. He is the nicest natured of my children. I am surprised, but deeply gratified, that you thought he took after me. Fair hair apart, he seems to have Fergus's disposition. I sometimes think he doesn't need fairy stories; he is supplied with a ready-made world of his own into which he can float away at will. A darling child, but I should feel easier could I detect a measure of Fergus's toughness in him. Fergus says I am never satisfied, I have my dream child and now all I want is that he come down to earth.

A prolonged delay in finishing this, the pattern of the coming months. There won't be many letters this year.

Bless you for what you have done for us, and your family for agreeing to part with you.

Love,

Constance

Sussex,
June, 1957

My dear Sheila,

We were delighted to receive your letter telling us that Linnie has been awarded a scholarship (or assisted place, as you refer to it). Fergus says we will have to build an extension to accommodate yet another photograph of the entire school; alternatively, he suggests a frieze around the sitting-room walls. A separate letter is enclosed for Linnie, together with a cheque from her proud godparent. I expect there will be all sorts of extras which she will need. Do they still play lacrosse?

Dominic takes the 11+ examination next year and if he passes will go to the Catholic grammar school. No amount of assistance would enable us to send him to an independent school. This success of Linnie's has had a noticeable effect on him. He is a boy who thrives on competition and can hardly forgive Linnie for being born before him.

Little other news from us. Fergus has provided himself with a small lab. in what was the potting shed. He goes out there to ponder when family life gets too much for him. As well as his scientific toys, he has installed a gramophone on which he plays classical music for the good of his soul and the bane of our neighbours. I hear doors and windows closing all down the road.

At this moment, I hear the twins yelling.

Love and rejoicing to you all,

Constance

My dear Sheila,

We managed it! No, we were not the people who arrived noisily late. We were in our seats – just – as the conductor raised his baton. There was no time to let you know we were coming and no time to see you afterwards because we came by train.

Fergus's parents are staying with us and then going on to his brother for Christmas (Fergus and his father are burning the midnight logs as I write). It is their first visit and we weren't sure how they would feel about our leaving them in charge so soon after their arrival. Fortunately, Fergus's father still has the appearance of being intimidating and his mother is prepared to be endlessly diverted by Stephen and the twins, so children of all ages were well catered for.

It was a splendid reception, wasn't it? We got very excited and squabbled all the way home because I preferred the *Tuileries* to *Conjunctions* and Fergus went so far as to say I had no appreciation of musical wit and, furthermore, that my taste is sentimental if not superficial. We were so excited by Miles's triumph.

From where I was sitting, I could see you quite clearly in the hoop of the hall. It's always a surprise to have those whom we take for granted cast off the homely wrappings to which we are accustomed and reveal themselves arrayed in splendour. Of course, if they make a mess of it, mismatched and garish, that presents us only with the duty of a little charity; but when splendour so becomes them as to make us feel we have never fully known them, a daunting generosity is required of us. You will realise I'm speaking of the black velvet dress and rainbow shawl and you so at one with them as to make a stranger believe you were ever thus. It wasn't so much that these trappings flattered, emphasised, highlighted, as that they proclaimed you. And now that I have made my obeisance, I don't want to be told that you contrived that glowing dress out of an old curtain or that your mother rescued the shawl from the dressing-up trunk which was our childhood delight.

I watched you during the interval. You were directing something that needed attention and you looked so assured among all those important people. I thought, the years have gone by and there has come into being a Sheila whom I do not know. It amazes me, this unlikely friendship. I give out so much nervous energy I should carry a warning that it is dangerous to come into contact with me; sparks fly from agitated fingers and tapping toes. You are still and composed, yet one is aware of a force within.

All in all, a considerable experience. Why only the two pieces? Why should Vaughan Williams and Delius share the evening with us?

Your admiring,
Constance

Sussex
June, 1958

My dear Sheila,

Harpo came, a plumped-up carrier pigeon bearing messages. I am envious that she sees more of you than I do.

I am told that during her stay with you Harpo witnessed Miles tearing up sheet after sheet of early compositions, not in temper, but attending to the matter with a kind of delicacy, fingers arched as if above the keyboard, the paper torn again and again until it was in tiny pieces. Harpo said she could have wept and to make good the omission she shed a few tears while she was telling us about it. I remember that you once said he had these destructive impulses. How could he throw away so much work, even if there were aspects which disappointed him? I, who create with such labour, would need to husband my output, however flawed. I gather that Harpo had the temerity to ask whether freedom from the wretched pupils was not worth some journeyman work and she painted a dramatic picture of you responding, throwing words like knives, 'He never compromises. I would leave him tomorrow were he to compromise', with which she was much impressed. To me, that has a theatricality I don't associate with you, a suggestion of desperation, even. Perhaps Harpo exaggerates.

I will tell you, since she certainly will when next she sees you, that I'm pregnant again. We had not intended it. A large family, five children perhaps, yes. Then came the twins and now an accident. Comments about football teams will not be welcome.

What other news? My agnostic vicar has left. I think he owes his preferment to the fact that he is too progressive for a backward rural area where people still believe in the Three Persons of the Trinity. To punish us, we have been sent an austere Evangelical fundamentalist. Fergus is despondent. He and the previous man talked for hours. Each was the kind of Christian who gets on better with people of other faiths or no faith at all.

Fergus says I expect too much of priests. 'You demand a messenger from Heaven, not an ordinary human being. You grumble that the Anglican Church is ill at ease with God and then, when you get a man who doesn't choose a breakfast cereal until he has prayed about it, that doesn't please you.'

It is true, I am very hard to please these days. How does one set about sweetening one's nature? Suggestions may not be well received.

Love,

Constance

Sussex
March, 1959

My dear Sheila,

Our grateful thanks for the presents, all of which much needed. I am particularly touched that Linnie made hers and have written to her separately. Peg is a very contented baby and lies for hours creating her world around her, seeing that it is good.

I ask myself what I have done to deserve so much good fortune. I love all my children, even Dominic, with whom I row incessantly, and Cuillane, my quiet child, who tends to drop out of sight. Perhaps Kathleen and Stephen are the ones dearest to my heart. They are so unlike me, she so open and fearless, not a devious bone in her body, and he so intermittently connected to planet earth and yet so kindly on the occasions when he does touch down. I love the twins, although to them I am only a provider of food. They are entirely absorbed in each other, two owlish lumps until I turn my back on them, when they proceed to lose themselves in mutual adoration.

I sometimes think that at heart I am still the only child playing a game in which she is a member of a large family. I remember I had a box full of plaits of different-coloured wool, nut brown, buttercup, orange – which I much preferred – and I tucked these behind my ears to denote which member of the family I was playing, whether Stephanie, Coralie or Marguerite. The boys (a cap stolen from a cousin instead of plaits) were Kit, Oliver and Philip. I hated being an only one. Dominic, Kathleen, Cuillane, Stephen, James, Gillian, Peg, they are not in the least like my childhood family, but I was right about needing them so much, only now they are not brothers and sisters but my children.

How I have rambled. A luxury. Fergus's brother and his wife are staying here. She is a prodigious worker and insisted on doing the washing and ironing this morning. This afternoon they have taken the children out, all except Peg who is busy creating the plants on the window-ledge. The house is so quiet I can hear someone mowing a lawn a field away.

You asked in your letter how Fergus's experiments were developing. Slowly, would be a fair assessment. He is working on something to do with soil improvement. Theoretically, he is overturning the Law of Diminishing Returns. The Byrnes should shortly become totally self-supporting and able to supply the entire neighbourhood.

I must now, with such vegetables as are at my disposal, prepare supper and attend to the needs of the last in the line.

It would be wonderful if you could get down here for a weekend, or even a day before the summer is over. It is so long since we had a sight of you.

    In hope and with love,
      Constance

My dear Sheila,

I'm sorry my notes have been so scrappy. It's been a bad year. Mumps, measles and nursing Aunt Ada, who returned home last week. Fortunately, I have my family well trained. 'As soon as they were on their feet, I gave them their roles,' I said to my vicar when he asked how I managed. I don't think he was best pleased. I was supposed to say love.

There has been one local development which will interest you. New people have moved into the house at the end of our road – the one you christened the Manderley of Sussex because it stands brooding behind tall trees. The people don't match up to the de Winter image. He is a small, oval man with dark, sleek hair and tragic monkey eyes who reminds me of George Raft. She is a fat, buttery blonde with tiny feet who tiptoes from front door to car. She never appears to be exposed to the fresh air for longer than three minutes at any one time. He is punctilious in his greetings, she apologetic.

My neighbour, Jenny Crow (Mrs Civil Servant) calls her the Baby Doll of Downland Way. They are the sort of people one thinks of in terms of other people, as they have no imprint of their own. They moved in just before Christmas but so far none of us has set foot inside the house. The Petersons, who live next door to them, say they are quiet as mice.

I have a theory they are as poor as church mice and desperately anxious that none should see the pictures hung over damp patches on walls, the chairs strategically placed to cover holes in the sitting-room carpet. I visualise them seated huddled in the kitchen because they cannot afford to heat the rest of the house.

'They are living beyond their means,' I said to Fergus.

He lost his temper and said we lived beyond our means and the whole of the English middle class did the same, throwing buckets of money around to ensure that the flowers in the border weren't shamed by the ones next door. Whereupon I became angry and said I was sick of the exiled Irish finding fault with the country that gave them their living. I went on to say that

I felt I had earned the right to live in Ireland so that I could daily descant upon its shortcomings and mourn the lost glories of my motherland. He said he would set about our move the very next day, whereupon Stephen and the twins began to cry and Cuillane got upset because Gus, our Labrador, is too elderly to survive such an upheaval even were we allowed to export him. Our guilt was compounded by Dominic saying to Cuillane, 'They don't mean it. Surely you know by now they don't mean anything they say.' We went to bed wretchedly aware that, as far as children are concerned, we are definitely living beyond our capabilities, to say nothing of our means.

I leave you in suspense as to the outcome. Will next year see the Byrne family in Sussex or Kilkenny? To be continued, probably for the rest of our lives.

Love,

Constance

P.S. The 11+ letter has arrived. Kathleen, like Toby, is a borderline candidate. Unlike Toby, she is adamant that she does not want to go to grammar school.

Sussex
May, 1960

My dear Sheila,

Et tu! What are we playing at, you ask, tossing aside so lightly this question of Kathleen's future schooling? I sit with bowed head while your wrath rains down upon me. Knowledge enabled man to climb out of the primeval sludge. Are you sure it wasn't a misdirected marine vertebrate? But I take your meaning. Education has been the most important single factor in improving the lives of millions in this century. Were it not for education you would be working the cabbage patch, indistinguishable from your great-grandmother and signing your name with a cross. Education has enabled common people to have some measure of control over their lives and has given them the chance of fulfilling their potential.

Are you quite done? May I speak?

Yes, we do appreciate that Kathleen has come to the great crossroads in a child's life. Before the fateful letter arrived we, too, asked ourselves whether she was to be one of the blessed 25 per cent sheep or the 75 per cent goats consigned to the educational wilderness. In fact, she has now been offered a grammar school place. But what is cause for rejoicing in the Druce household has seen the opening of hostilities here. You say that the fact that Linnie is doing so well influenced the selection panel in Toby's favour. Toby is obviously less resentful of favours than Kathleen, who informed us she was not going to pass her time at secondary school 'trying to live down Dominic'.

We did take our responsibilities seriously, I assure you. Night after night we sat up in bed asking ourselves what we considered to be the main function of education. Did we, like our friends and neighbours, believe that academic success was of paramount importance? Admittedly, our discussion lacked something of your passionate conviction, but then we neither of us see our local secondary school as in any way related to primeval sludge. And we did agree that we would like success for our children, but as a bonus rather than an essential. So what was essential? There, I have to admit, we lacked your clarity of thought. I said I would like Kathleen to be enabled to find herself and you will be pleased to know that Fergus asked what I thought that meant. I could only answer that my own education had tended in the direction of moulding rather than finding with the result that I still have grave doubts as to who I am. Fergus said I reduced all discussion to the personal. I said I would like education to be more concerned with the personal. Fergus considered Kathleen as a person. 'She is naturally adventurous. I wouldn't want others to set her sights for her.' In the early hours, when he was making tea, he said wearily, 'How are we to persuade her to give it a try when we ourselves are so hopelessly lacking in conviction?'

Kathleen had all the advantage of absolute certainty. 'Cuillane is bound to be an under-age candidate and then I'll have years of her in the same school. I can't compete with Cuillane. At least with Dominic anyone can see how hard he tries to be clever, but she doesn't have to try.'

'But suppose the others all go to grammar school?' Fergus said. 'In later life you may feel at a great disadvantage.'

'Stephen will probably go into a trance during the tests. As for the twins, they're as thick as two planks; you'll have to send them to a special school.'

'But your friends,' I persisted. 'Doreen Ellis and . . .'

'Stella Pierce is going to the secondary modern and she's the only one I care about. As soon as the results came out, the others changed . . .'

I consulted the Headmistress of Kathleen's primary school. She has quite a reputation and people will consider moving house in order to ensure that their children attend her school. I think this is because she manages to uphold the old traditions while giving an appearance of being able to square up to anything the modern world can throw at her. She is the mistress of paradox, a woman in whom virtue is delightfully combined with a certain naughtiness and common sense seems not incompatible with idealism. She is plump and dyes her hair salmon. Her skin is prawn mottled with cinnamon. She wears brightly coloured clothes and looks a bit brassy, but cheerful and sturdy with it, like a Renoir barmaid. She's not a woman whose geese are all swans, so I was heartened when she said that Kathleen probably had more practical intelligence than Cuillane. 'Academically, of course, she won't go so far, but I don't think you need fear that she will limp along in the C stream of a grammar school. She might well get a university placement, not Oxbridge, of course.' She folded her fat little hands and contemplated the array of rings which formed two jewelled knuckle-dusters. 'But, having said all that, I have to admit to reservations about her suitability. She has a strong personality and she is a natural leader. She might realise her full potential at the top of a good secondary modern school rather than being an also-ran at the grammar school. Much depends on how you and your husband feel about it.'

I confessed I had been brought up in the belief that grammar schools laid more emphasis on character building. Her eyes popped wide open. 'That was a very long time ago, Mrs Byrne, back in the days of Miss Beale and Miss Buss.'

I muttered something about values.

'Ah, now! Values.' She patted her hands on the table and light sparked from the rings. She was enjoying this vastly; it was as though she recognised in me a rare stone to add to her collection. 'What values, Mrs Byrne? You assume a society which has common values, do you?'

I searched round for a few values with which to dazzle her. 'Caring about the community in which one lives, public service, considering one's neighbours even if one can't love them, being a responsible citizen.'

She clapped her hands. 'Yes, yes, how well I recall my own headmistress telling us that the purpose of our education was to make us into good citizens of our country.'

'I know it sounds rather lame,' I said, 'but if you do away with that kind of concern, society will lose a lot.'

'You know what they will say to you? "Citizens of what country?" The country you inhabit isn't the same country that the miner inhabits, or the coloured bus conductor. Not that I have any personal experience of either.' She said this in the same tone in which Gwendolen Fairfax disclaimed acquaintance with a spade. 'But it's what they say, these people just down from university, who, let's face it, Mrs Byrne, are going to shape the schools of the future. Their question to you would be – whose values?'

'Middle-class values.'

'One can't rely on the middle class any more, I'm afraid. Success is all that most of them want for their children. Service is a word not much used now.'

'I seem to be rather out of date.'

'We both are, my dear. I have quite settled for being a relic.'

That was all very well for her, single, roguishly eccentric and in her fifties. It is early in life for me to be outdated. I suppose it is the war which has been the great divide. Was there a line we failed to hold while we were busy defeating the Germans?

'It's not my values as such which concern me,' I said later to Fergus. 'I'm sure all values need to be taken out and re-examined from time to time and those which haven't worn well thrown away to make room for new ones. What bothers me is that it should no longer be appropriate, in fact should be slightly disreputable, to admit to values of any kind.'

'It's all a matter of vocabulary,' he said. 'Values out, relativity in.'

We spent another night propped up on pillows meditating on such questions as can success be equated with fulfilment? and is the possession of a university degree essential to achievement? We didn't seem to arrive at any conclusions, but the next morning we were both convinced that Kathleen would not be happy at grammar school and that she is not sufficiently interested in academic success to do well in adverse conditions.

So, there it is, Sheila. In September Kathleen will go to the local secondary modern school. It has a nice new building on the outskirts of the village and the Headmaster is very affable. Our friends think we have made a dreadful mistake. Fergus's priest disapproves because although the grammar school is RC the secondary modern is undenominational. So her soul is in jeopardy as well as her mind.

And you? Will you forgive us?

In hope,

Constance

Sussex
January, 1961

My dear ageing friend,

Our fortieth year – all four of us in our forties. Fergus in fact, balanced twixt forty and fifty. He sustains it well enough. His face is nobbly and his hair is sparse but standing up for itself here and there. He still has those long-distance eyes but the whites are getting pinkish and I tell him he had better cut down on the drink before the veins get to be broken.

Would it be possible for you all to come down here, either on my birthday, or yours, for a huge family celebration? If this doesn't appeal, could we meet in London, the four of us, for a celebratory meal? Do try.

 Love,
  Constance

P.S. Isn't it exciting that America has this new young President? What is all this nonsense about ageing at forty?

Sussex
August, 1961

My dear Sheila,

We should have done it years ago. Miles is much better at celebrating than I had imagined. In fact, I don't think I have ever before met anyone who became more witty the more he drank. Fergus, like most men, comes out with stories he wouldn't have told when sober and doesn't tell very well when drunk.

When we came out of the station it was a beautiful night with a great moon the colour of Dutch cheese. We were so happy we decided to leave the car and walk home. Soon I became painfully aware of not wearing the right shoes, so I took them off and we walked across the fields singing 'Tiptoe through the tulips' and 'She'll be coming round the mountain' (naval words) and started all the farm dogs barking. Then Fergus rebuked them, 'Be not afeard; the isle is full of noises, Sounds and sweet airs, that give delight and hurt not.' But the very sound of the human voice convinced them they were right to be afeard. Reaching the gate leading into our road, Fergus turned to assure them, 'Our revels now are ended . . .'. He did the whole speech quite beautifully, but they were not to be comforted. As we lay in bed Fergus said, 'How beauteous mankind is! O brave new world that has such people in't!' Alas, came morning with sound and fury because he had to get a taxi to the station.

I have a slight headache. How are you and Miles?

 Love,
  Constance

My dear Sheila,

Thank you for your generous offer. I hadn't meant to drop a hint when I said we were looking for suitable activities to occupy Dominic, Kathleen and Cuillane while the rest of us went to Ireland. I was thinking in terms of an adventure camp for Dominic and something a bit less rigorous for the girls. If you and Miles really think you can cope, we should be very grateful.

Shall I give you a bit of advice which you may or may not wish to take? It is a scheme which has worked well on past holidays. Devise a points system – so many points for help in preparing food, washing up, bed-making and any other chores you wish to include. You will find Dominic an absolute treasure. His determination to come first in everything quite blinds him to the fact that he is doing more work than anyone else.

Should you have second thoughts, important engagements, or whatever else, please let us know.

Our love and thanks,
Constance

County Wicklow
August, 1962

My dear Sheila,

We have received a letter from Kathleen telling us that your father met them at Victoria and took them home with him to Ealing. She says it wasn't convenient for you to have them. Something is wrong. Are you ill? Or Miles? Or has something happened to one of the children? Do please let us know, even if you only send a p.c.

Anxiously,
Constance

My darling Sheila,

I have read your letter through and through. Surely it is one of those anxiety dreams and I shall wake soon. There have been times when I wouldn't have blamed Fergus had he taken flight, but that it should happen to you is inconceivable. You sound so calm, trying to be fair to this little trollop, Joey. My poor Linnie, to have her father made a fool by a girl only a year older than herself. Had you any inkling of what was going on during her lessons?

She isn't pregnant, I suppose? That might make for complications. But eventually he must come back. You have all given him so much; he couldn't throw away such joy. You were my dream family. When I was tired and fractious and couldn't sleep at night, I used to close my eyes and see you all in that great barn of a room, making music together. As I lay listening every wrinkle was ironed out. This was the threshold of Heaven and I imagined the music and the music makers to be one. It's a brainstorm. He has always been precariously balanced, a likely subject for middle-age madness. It will pass. You would have him back, wouldn't you? We have always said that we would never show the children the door whatever they might do and that we would have the man back were he to stray. Too much goes into the making of a marriage, sheer hard work apart from anything else, to throw it away for the sake of pride and you have never been proud.

Your parents must be heart-broken. Fergus is writing to them. Will you let me know how Linnie and Toby are taking this. Would it help if I wrote to them?

My love, you must feel so wounded and baffled. When we return, if he hasn't regained his senses, come, all of you and we'll weep and rage together.

Our dearest love,
Constance

County Wicklow
August, 1962

Sheila, my dear,

Yes, since you demand truthfulness, that ugly blight, I was surprised by your saying you would not have Miles back. What particularly disturbed me was that you sounded as if you had been forming this decision over a long period. I could understand your pacing the house, crying out, 'I will never have him back, never, not even were he to crawl all the way from Kew Gardens station.' But I can't understand this calm appraisal of the situation, gathering together past and present, this cool resolve that the future shall be quite other. I would always have Fergus back – I may already have had him back for all I know in my innocence.

Nowadays there is a tendency to throw away the rule book, to allow our wishes and needs to be the rules of the moment. You were never like that. You have put so much of yourself into this marriage; love and patience, laughter and tears, learning and forgiving have gone to the making of it. Remember the good years as well as the bad. Miles has been foolish, but we love our men for their weaknesses as much as their strengths, don't we? Indeed, were we ourselves to be loved only for our strengths, what hope would we have?

And what of the children? You yourself once said they lived in a sealed chamber with you and Miles with the result that they made few friends. How will they manage when they have been brought up to despise the very skills which they will now need?

Don't think I'm judging you, my love; this is a plea not to be too hasty, not to do anything that would make Miles feel there is no way back.

My love and prayers,
Constance

My dearest Sheila,

I found your letter hurtful and put it aside until we returned home. You were very abrupt on the telephone last night and I suspect you're still angry with me.

Can it really seem to you that I scarcely remember who you are, have not, in fact, seen you very clearly since that class photograph was taken? Oh dear, how much self-examination this has brought about! I am afraid it's only too true that I tend to read my meanings into your sentences. No wonder you found it necessary to state your feelings about Miles so bluntly.

I can see, looking back, that for years I have been presenting you with my view of your life. It seemed to me that you were uniquely fortunate in having such a close, all-embracing relationship. You're right. As the walls went up around you, I stood by and applauded. I did indeed find cause for congratulation in the disorderly house, the wild garden, the empty hearth and the untimely meals. Though I do remember that once – I don't recall in what connection – I detected a hint of desperation in you and I think I commented on it. You never responded.

I have one memory of Miles which recurs disturbingly. I once had tea with him in a café in Cambridge. Perhaps I told you about it. The waitress was little more than a child; a thin, undernourished creature looking at him with the rapacious eyes of the willing slave to whom servitude, even of the most abject kind, gives sustenance. Can this be what he secretly desires in a woman?

I wish you had told me that from the very beginning there was trouble between you and Miles. The fact that he was possessive did not escape me, but I even envied you that. 'You wouldn't care if you knew that you weren't the first love of my life, would you?' I once said to Fergus. I don't recall his reply, probably because it was non-committal.

How different we are! You say you loved Miles because there was something that meant more to him than you. His consuming passion was music. You like that kind of passion in a man. I, on the other hand, much regret the tendency in Fergus to look to something beyond the bend in the road, the brow of the hill. He will never tell me what it is, he probably doesn't know himself, but it's there, somewhere in the distance in a place where I'm not. This kind of passion in a man does not please me.

I'm disturbed by the things you say. There is another person in all of us, 'a dark presence waiting in the wings, ready to take over in time of emergency'. I have sometimes been made aware, mostly in dreams, of another person in me with whom I don't want to have much to do. Unlike you, I don't care for this word emergency – emergence, emerge, something humbler than advent, yet a coming to being none the less. I tremble for you. Miles has unlocked a door.

Although you were so annoyed with me, you seemed concerned about my children. They are shocked, even Dominic is subdued. Kathleen is angry. Cuillane spends some time explaining to Stephen. He and she are great friends and I think it helps her to talk to him. I heard her say yesterday, 'Yes, he still loves Auntie Sheila. The trouble is, he loves too many people.'

It seems strange to me that your one feeling of guilt should be that you may have caused my children to question the security of their own home. What of your children, Sheila? You say that you would die for them but are not prepared to sacrifice yourself for them day by day. Are they to be left to rub along as best they can?

We must talk about these things. As soon as term begins it should be possible for me to come up to see you. In the meantime, let me know if there is anything we can do.

Our love to you all,
Constance

Sussex
September, 1962

My dear Sheila,

We will certainly have Linnie, if you really think it wise to separate from the children; at a time when they have lost one parent it may be more than they can bear to lose the other. Why not stay on in the house until they are both through school and then start to look for somewhere else to live?

Fergus thinks it will be a long time before you can sort out the legal situation regarding property. In his opinion, it would be unwise to do anything which would suggest you were prepared to accommodate yourself to Miles's arrangements. I pointed out that, far from being accommodating, you couldn't wait to live an independent life and he said there was no reason why you shouldn't be independent and still have a roof over your head and assisted school places for the children. 'There is a battle ahead of her, but at least she occupies the castle and it is Miles who must do the besieging. I don't see him making a good job of that. I wouldn't back him to get one piano, let alone a harp, out of that house without doing himself a mischief. And while she can't pour boiling oil over him from an upstairs window, more's the pity, she can make sure his progress is impeded by every legal means available to her.' He suggests we should come up for the day next weekend to talk things over.

Oh, how this has rocked my own small boat! I look at Fergus and wonder what he may have done and can't bring myself to ask for fear that, whatever he might reply, I would know the answer as I looked into his face.

Our love and prayers,
Constance

Sussex
September, 1962

My dear Sheila,

I learnt a great deal from our talk. As I listened to you in that room which I had always imagined to be the still centre of your lives, I realised this was something which always had to happen. If not now, then later, Miles would destroy his happiness.

When you told us that love represented a threat to him because one day the thread from which it hung must break, I remembered how nervous he was when Linnie was a baby. He said to me before the christening, 'If you dropped her, she would smash to pieces.' I sympathised with him then because babies seemed to me to be all too breakable; I have since learnt that they are remarkably tough. But perhaps this is how Miles felt all the time – that nothing is tough enough to survive the ticking of a clock.

I can understand that the one thing which enabled you to continue to respect him was his music. For him, it must have represented a triumph over almost impossible odds to impose form and order, like working on a diamond knowing that one ill-judged blow can shatter the whole. Whenever I listen to *Last Thoughts in the Tuileries Gardens* I shall marvel at how the human spirit can rise above its handicaps and compose, out of jangling pain and tumult, such calm, ordered beauty.

On the way home, Fergus stopped the car near Richmond Bridge and we walked along the towpath, although it was nearly dark and raining hard. I think he was gasping for air and I found myself putting out my tongue to catch the raindrops. What haunted Fergus was your description of the many days when Miles would follow you around the house demanding information about something he imagined to be worrying Linnie, or alienating Toby, refusing to be reassured, asking where you were going, what you were doing, why did this or that have to be attended to at a time when he needed your undivided attention, his questions moulding a pitch-cap to your head until the lavatory and a plea of constipation became your only refuge. 'He wanted to be in every moment of her life,' Fergus said. 'Another person can be the most effective form of prison.' The river was black and flowing out fast and I think we both wished we could deliver you to it and let it carry you far away from that house and its bitter memories. I had noticed that all the windows in the house were open and I hoped that perhaps, even as we stood there, you might be leaning out and could just discern the dark glint of water.

The town soon slips away as one walks and there was an island, a dense mass of drenched trees, which blotted out the lights of the distant houses. The only sound was the squelch of our inadequately shod feet in spongy ground and the slopping of driftwood in the reeds. One can make what one will, according to mood, of the smell that comes up from the river. I was aware of the broken things it carries, putrefied by their long immersion. It came to me, watching the river, how much of my own life had flowed by, its passage unheeded, nothing of moment achieved. All sorts of questions hovered in the air which it would not have been wise to ask. What was Fergus thinking? I could see his silhouette, the rain streaming down his face as he stared across to the island, and for a moment he was a stranger, some stranded mariner trying to identify an unfamiliar shore. Was he asking, 'How came I to be washed up here?' Did he feel that in his life with me much had gone to waste? As night came we walked back. It was so dark, that water. The rain had got under the collar of my jacket and an icy trickle ran down my spine. If anything dreadful were ever to happen to me, I have a fear I might wade into that dark water. I wouldn't have your strength in adversity.

If ever you think it would help Linnie or Toby to get away from the house, you know you can send them to us. Linnie was raw with grief, but there was a blankness in Toby's eyes I did not like to see. It might do him good to be with our brood for a few days; the young have their own way of helping one another.

Let me know when you have talked things over with brother Angus. I am so glad that he is going to act for you.

Our love and blessings,

Constance

Sussex
January, 1963

My dear Sheila,

How cruel that it should be on Boxing Day, when we looked forward to having the three of you and your parents here, that Sussex should be obliterated along with the rest of the country. 'It never happens here,' our neighbours assure us as we fight to keep our nostrils above the snow line. 'It never comes this far south in Sussex.'

My mother and Aunt Ada managed to get away on the 29th. Indeed, by now you have probably received graphic accounts of their stay, though delicacy may prevent their telling how Aunt Ada gallantly insisted on carrying the laden lavatory bucket out to the garden only to have the handle break when she was half-way down the stairs. Fergus and I were alerted to the state of affairs by Dominic howling, 'We shall all have typhoid!'

We have had another heavy fall this morning. I do not like this whiteness. Fergus took Dominic, Kathleen and Cuillane to school after he had dug the car out of the garage. I watched them dissolve in whiteness and wondered if I would ever see them again. Stephen and the twins went off on a tractor. Their school is quite near so I feel they are retrievable. The sky is sickly grey above the dazzling white. Already a few flakes are falling.

Peg and the dogs frolic. The cats hate it; they stand in the doorway, fastidious paws raised, and complain as if I were responsible. What the rabbits make of it I don't know because I haven't yet burrowed my way to them. Before I do any work, before I even decide which of all the many challenges to meet first – shall it be digging a path to the coal shed, putting the oil stove in the lavatory in the hope of unfreezing the cistern, emptying the linen cupboard because any thaw in whatever part of the house always results in a burst pipe and piles of wet sheets – before I do any of these things, I am determined to get a letter off to you. This is such a wearying time, even the simplest task taking twice as long, to say nothing of the frozen brain working so slowly, and it must be trebly hard for you, exhausted by worry and sorrow. There, I have done it again! Why is it that I cannot stop telling you how you are feeling? The fact is I am having a struggle to adjust to this new life of yours. I still see you in the days when you and Miles were together. As a child, it always took me a long time to acclimatise to a change of air. Bear with me.

As soon as the weather relents and you feel you can leave the house without fear of its turning into a block of ice, you must all come down for a weekend. Do you promise?

Our love to you all and come soon,

Constance

P.S. The people in the Manderley house went out on Christmas Day and were unable to get back. The ground slopes so steeply the snow was up to the window-sills. Fergus and some of the other men went to offer assistance when they returned, but they refused all help. She was quite distraught. I now have a theory that she is mentally retarded and he can't bear that anyone should know.

Sussex
April, 1963

My dear Sheila,

It was a surprise to hear your news when you stayed with us last month. There was I picturing you engaged in a dour battle with the house when in fact you were slogging purposefully through the snow to these interviews at the Education Office. How brave you are! When Dominic and Kathleen start talking about their school work I dare not open my mouth, such is the extent of my ignorance; but you listened to our young with that enjoyment which can only come of the confident knowledge that one has a trick or two up one's sleeve. I'm sure you will make a very good teacher.

We enjoyed having you all here. Linnie looked pale and listless, I thought. Be patient with her, my love. I know her indecisiveness can be irritating, but she hasn't your resilience. Toby worries me. It was kind of him to play games with Stephen and to amuse the twins, but I would have been happier had he kept company with the older ones. We didn't have much time to talk about the suggestion that he should see the educational psychologist, but I got the impression you were not very happy about it. I'm glad he is seeing more of your father; I would put my money on him rather than any psychologist.

We have our struggles here. Fergus is much dismayed by this talk at the Vatican Council of the use of vernacular liturgies. It comes hard to the Irish, struggling to revive one dead language and now finding themselves deprived of another. Why is it that one can't preserve the glories of the past while setting one's face to the future? It seems to be one of the laws of life that thou shalt not have it both ways. I hope and trust that one of the wonders of the world to come will be having it all ways.

I tell Fergus that if language is all he has to bother about he can count himself lucky; it is as nothing to the storm we Anglicans must brace ourselves for as a result of this *Honest to God* book. Have you read it? I gather he actually refers to Christians who think of God as an old man with a long white beard. It does make one wonder what kind of world our bishops inhabit that this is their picture of the people in the pews.

I have found consolation in Baron von Hügel's letters to a niece. Have you come across them? I was spring-cleaning Fergus's study, as we are pleased to call that little cell between the dining-room and the scullery, when I swept one too many a book from the shelf. It fell at my feet. I shall always regard it as a small miracle that it did not fall open at a page where he is pontificating about the Odes of Pindar, or protesting that he doesn't want to convert his niece to the Roman Church when to the reader it stands out all too clearly that this is what he is bursting to do. Rather, I found myself reading 'Never try to get things too clear. In this mixed up life there is always an element of unclearness.' What words to stare out at me at a time when I find myself pestered by people who want to tidy up my mind. He says of people who seek to know God exhaustively, 'they are like sponges trying to mop up the ocean'. I began to read and was still curled up on the floor with the book on my lap when Peg came back from playgroup.

I have read and reread, skipping the bits about literature and the Roman Church. The spiritual advice is pure gold. Why did no one ever tell me these things before? Drop, ignore antipathies, do not strive to like people or to be like someone else. I have spent years striving to like and be like. Some people are born good-natured and positively enjoy being kind and charitable, but my natural bent is towards ill nature. For years I have struggled with this problem. Somewhere, so deep inside me I know not whence it comes, there is a voice forever telling me, 'You must struggle against this, Constance.' Now comes the suggestion that perhaps more might be achieved by making less of it. He is the first person who has ever introduced me to a way of thinking about my religion that was not totally effortful – the kind of enterprise one goes about with elbows out, as if spring-cleaning. Be silent about great things, let them grow inside you. Never discuss them. . . . One of the verses in the Bible which I have always loved, though I never thought to associate it with my own living, is 'Mary kept all these things, and pondered them in her heart.' I feel as I read that he understands how I tend to get my teeth into a subject and worry at it like a terrier, and that if I am very attentive he may be able to help me as well as his niece.

I must work in the garden now. How blessed it is to have the green world restored to us. I am determined our garden shall send up loud hosannas – which it will do without my aid; the daffodils were proclaiming the glory of the Lord while Fergus and I were squabbling over whether it was necessary for him to paint the garden tools yet again.

Let me know if you decide to let Toby see the educational psychologist.

My love to you all,
Constance

Sussex
July, 1963

My dear Sheila,

Yes, I can understand how this new work eats up your energy. I will be patient and content myself with a postcard here and there and such other crumbs as may fall from the staffroom table.

There is one thing, however, on which I would be grateful for your comments when you have time to write. Have you come across any evidence of drug-taking since you have been teaching? I ask because a friend of Dominic's was at a party where there was trouble with the neighbours which led to the police being called. As a result several people were arrested for smoking what Dominic referred to as 'pot' and I have always thought of as 'reefers'. Admittedly, this happened in Notting Hill, where the friend's elder brother has digs. But Dominic does see rather a lot of this family and was obviously impressed by the pot-smoking elder brother.

'It's nothing to get so excited about,' he said to us. 'People have been using marijuana down the ages.'

'People may have done,' Fergus said, 'but the Byrnes haven't.'

'It's probably less harmful than alcohol,' Dominic persisted.

'Have you smoked a reefer?' I asked.

'*Reefer!* Oh, Mother!' He went out of the room, banging the door behind him.

'Do you think he has?' I asked Kathleen.

'Day and night,' she said.

This was as far as we could get. The children thought it a great joke and for several days we had to bear with Stephen's impersonation of a Somerset Maugham character.

I spoke to the mother of the pot-smoking young man. She is one of those advanced women who believe that children should be free to experiment. 'People in this country are so ignorant about drugs that they are incapable of making sensible judgements. Pot isn't habit-forming and it has no bad after-effects.'

I am not persuaded. Any advice will be welcome.

Our love to you all,
Constance

Sussex
November, 1963

My dear Sheila,

I was in the kitchen, rolling pastry, and Kathleen and Cuillane were peeling vegetables. One of them switched on the radio and we heard a voice say, 'It is not thought that the

President was hurt.' We all froze as if we were playing statues and the music had stopped. Kathleen had a curl of potato peel on the knife. A voice said that an appeal had gone out for blood. Then the news came to an end and a different voice announced that President Kennedy was dead. Kathleen burst into tears; she is the one of all my children who has perfect emotional pitch. Dominic, who appeared a few minutes later, was consumed with personal outrage because to him Kennedy represented the hope that the affairs of the world may one day be ordered by young men. Cuillane's reaction came later. 'He had only just begun.' She looked at me, explaining, 'Lincoln had finished, but he had only just begun.' I did not know what to say, my mind full of images of blood and poor Mrs Kennedy. She went on, speaking in the studious tone in which she discusses her homework with Fergus, 'I hadn't realised, I hadn't understood it could happen like that,' as if she had found a flaw in a mathematical formula which invalidated any conception of the constant order of phenomena. I so seldom see Cuillane clearly; pale and unemphatic, I suspect she prefers to be overlooked. There is never any suggestion that she feels neglected or would have things other than they are. I noticed on this occasion, however, that although she is so colourless, she is not insubstantial. No lack of purpose went to the making of that long face, the bones are those of the Celtic saints. It crossed my mind that she might become a nun.

I should have spoken to Fergus about her later. He has a closer relationship with her than I have. But we listened to the radio and time slipped by. After the last news bulletin we got the late-night reading, a man's voice, lilting:

'And as I was green and carefree, famous among the barns
About the happy yard and singing as the farm was home,
    In the sun that is young once only,
      Time let me play and be
    Golden in the mercy of his means,
And green and golden I was huntsman and herdsman, the
   calves

Sang to my horn, the foxes on the hills barked clear and
   cold,
                  And the sabbath rang slowly
            In the pebbles of the holy streams.'

It was unbearable, to hear that morning song at such a time.

Your story haunts me, the empty tube station and the voice
calling to you from the cubby-hole, 'President Kennedy has
been shot.' How isolated that ticket collector must have felt,
holed up alone with such dark thoughts. Your gesture of
bringing the thermos flask of tea must have done much to warm
his heart.

Thank you for your comments on the drug question. I expect
you're right. Drug-taking isn't a mainline activity in our culture
and, even in his vices, Dominic is conventional.

I look forward to having you all at Christmas.

   Our love,
            Constance

Sussex
February, 1964

My dear Sheila,

   I know we decided, as you are so busy with school work, to
write less often. But I must forestall the report which Harpo will
undoubtedly send to you, she being with us at the time.

Miles came with that creature of his. I opened the door and
there he stood, this wisp of a thing at his side. He didn't
introduce her and she said, 'I'm Joey'; a reminder that an
addition had to be made to the cast list rather than a friendly
gesture. She was ageless, with close-cropped curly hair and a
greyish face with teeth to match; she could as easily have been
his son as his mistress. They had come in an ancient Armstrong
Siddeley which was blocking the driveway next door and when
I pointed this out, it was she who moved it. She did not look full-
grown enough to get her feet to the pedals; but she had the kind
of determination that can master any obstacle that gets in the

way of achievement. She treated the gears and clutch with that mixture of respect and contempt I associate with lion-tamers.

Fergus had appeared by now and was all for sending them packing; but as I had insisted on their reparking the car we could hardly refuse to admit them.

They sat close together on the sofa like children. Sheila, this is how he seemed to me, a wilful child who had, all unknowingly, started a process which is irreversible. He did not look happy. I recall that when he was amused he glittered, but did he ever look happy? Now there is no question of it. He has definitely settled into a state of unhappiness; but this, rather than turning him against Joey, seems to have made him pathetically dependent on her. She did not speak, just sat quietly with her knees drawn close, like a Victorian miss, watching him slantwise. She has stubby hands, the nails chipped, the cuticles ingrained with dirt; the sort of hands which are used to being in control of matter. While he was talking she kneaded the palms. Her eyes never left his face. I think she willed him into this affair.

He said, as if it caused him pain and surprise, that he had heard nothing from you. Harpo suggests he was surprised not to have been rescued by now. 'And my children,' he said. 'I don't know what is happening to my dear children.'

Harpo said, 'You don't think the children might have expected to hear from you?' as if she herself were unsure whether this were a reasonable expectation. Since taking up psychology direct questions are definitely out as far as Harpo is concerned. Miles did not respond to the indirect approach. I wanted to shout, 'Why haven't you tried to see your children?' As this may not be a development you would welcome, I held my peace. For what seemed a very long time we all held our peace. Then Miles burst into tears. Fergus said, 'Dear God, spare us this!' I went into the kitchen to make tea, which is my answer to situations that are too embarrassing to be borne. Harpo tells me that Joey held him to her as if about to breast-feed him.

As they were leaving, I said to him, and I hope you will forgive me, 'When are you going to stop this silliness and go back home?' I ignored her, but there was no need, she stood passively by without betraying the slightest uneasiness. He looked at me as if he were drowning and I his last hope. 'How can I?' Then, briskly, and with a different emphasis, 'How can I?' He took her hand and they stood there, holding hands, defying us. You are right, there is more than a streak of self-destructiveness in Miles; he does feel he has to kick down his building blocks.

Fergus went into the garden after they had gone and wreaked havoc among the vegetables. The children came out of the various parts of the house in which they had taken refuge and I left Harpo to deal with their enquiries while I washed the tea things. Later, when we were preparing supper, I said to Harpo, 'Yet he can't be completely under her control. He must have insisted on coming here. I don't see her suggesting it.'

Harpo said he wouldn't have had to insist; she would never thwart him. 'If he wanted them to dance naked in Piccadilly Circus, that little bitch would do it.'

'What did he expect of this visit?' I asked. 'Did he hope that if he managed to get here, he would find himself reinstated like the Prodigal Son, the past miraculously cancelled out?' Harpo said that he was genuinely troubled about you and the children and wanted to speak your names among friends. She talked a lot about guilt and the need for reassurance.

Whatever the reason, it may result in his writing to you or trying to get in touch with the children. This happened so unexpectedly, Sheila; we were none of us prepared and may have botched it badly. We were careful not to give him much in the way of information; but Fergus did tell him that you were teaching and he made it clear that this meant more to you than a matter of earning a few pence. It came as a surprise to Miles; I could see he had not envisaged your making a new life for yourself. Perhaps he had thought of you walled up in perpetual grief, perhaps that is what he wanted to think. It was soon after this that they left us.

My love, I hope this is not too upsetting for you and that it won't lead to unpleasant developments. We did our best on the spur of the moment.

     With love and some anxiety,

      Constance

Sussex
February, 1964

My dear Sheila,

     Thank you for your letter. I was sure you would want a full account, but I was afraid I might have said too much. I can see now that in my anxiety I may have painted a clearer picture of Joey than of Miles. You ask how he looked.

     He still had the appearance of not fitting into his surroundings and making it seem the surroundings which were at fault. Our sitting-room has not withstood the ravages of childhood assault and homely is the best one can say for it; yet he contrived to appear gaunt and awkward as a man returned from the mission field, unaccustomed to the comforts of Western society. To continue the religious theme, he still had that hungry look, the sort of hunger earthly food will not satisfy, which would make a saint of him were it not for the suspicion that Divine food would appeal to him even less. So, in that respect, she has not so much changed as allowed him to exacerbate his more extreme tendencies. I suspect that not only will she not thwart him, she will never apply a brake.

     Facially, there is a difference. It is not simply that his face is more deeply striated, time would have seen to that anyway. It is the eyes. Miles may have looked on the world without much liking, but he did find it a source of devilish glee. Now, the eyes stared unblinkingly, as if, just beyond where his feet rested, a great rift had opened up. He seemed, more often than not, to be addressing that void rather than anyone in the room. Perhaps it's that while he was safe with you he regarded the world as an entertainment; now it has ceased to entertain.

     I showed this letter to Fergus in case he had anything to add. He said Miles was an egoist and this explained the hungry look;

he had never had much in the way of nourishment to offer himself and his food store is therefore being depleted day by day. Fergus thinks you are well rid of Miles.

I am disappointed that you can't come at half-term; but I do appreciate that our house is not the quietest of places in which to study. Linnie and Toby will be very welcome; but do please look after yourself. Left alone, I fear you will go cold and unfed. Remember that if you deny yourself food and warmth your brain won't function so well.

  Love and admonitions,
    Constance

Sussex
October, 1964

My dear Sheila,

  When I felt the weight of your letter, I hoped that here was good news about the divorce and the sale of the house.

I am so distressed for you. As if you hadn't enough trouble without this pestilential psychiatrist. You don't say why it was decided to refer Toby to him. Was this the recommendation of the educational psychologist? It's all a plot to keep themselves in business.

Does this man have children of his own? How would he feel, rehearsing his troubles in front of a monosyllabic, enigmatic, uninvolved, grey-suited icon who showed great reluctance to take any part in moving the discussion along and who treated him like a complaining customer who had pushed past the sales assistant and stormed the manager's office? No wonder you felt as if Toby were a piece of equipment which had left the maker in good condition and must subsequently have been damaged in the home. It may well be important for Toby to feel that there is someone 'to whom he can talk about himself in absolute confidentiality, secure in the understanding that adverse comments are not being fed in without his knowledge'. Wouldn't we all love such a confidante? No wonder Toby bounces in like someone who has had a splendid evacuation when he returns

116

from a session; but most purgatives carry a warning that if the problem doesn't clear up within a few days one should consult a doctor. How is he to be helped by someone who has to rely for his assessment of the family situation on the impressions of a very disturbed youth? Is he God? Does he ever pause to wonder whether it is justifiable to encourage Toby to lay bare his feelings of resentment and to voice his belief that you are responsible for the loss of his father?

How dare he make you see yourself as a tough, unsympathetic mother! But are you quite sure this is, in fact, what he was saying? I know how sharply I react to criticism and if anyone were to say to me 'Do you think it is possible you may have failed to notice how quiet Cuillane is – or how strident Kathleen has become', I should immediately translate this into an accusation that I was a selfish, uncaring woman and unfit to be a mother. You are much more level-headed, but the past few years have been a struggle for you and any negative comment on the way in which you have coped is bound to be particularly wounding.

Yes, we will have Linnie at half-term, if you think this will help. Alternatively, why not send Toby? It might do him good to be here with Fergus, since he is missing the company of an older man. This would give Linnie time alone with you. I know you don't want her to become too dependent, but she is very attached to you and one can't push them into self-reliance before they are ready. Have a think about it.

It may cheer you to know that you are not alone in having trouble with your offspring. Dominic has been smoking pot. How exemplarily calm that sounds. We found out about it a couple of months ago, at which time calm I was not. Fergus and I were at odds as to the best way of dealing with him. I thought Fergus was too easy-going and he said that if I would persist in behaving as if Dominic had already blighted his life there would be no incentive for him to mend his ways.

My mother, who was staying with us, was surprisingly supportive. 'At least he didn't learn that at home,' she said, but could not forbear adding, 'Now, if it had been drink . . .'

Dominic insisted that he had not, in fact, smoked pot. He couldn't make up his mind whether to say this in court, thus letting his friends down – and possibly not being believed anyway – or admit to something he hadn't done and accept whatever the beaks handed out. In the event, he pleaded guilty because he thought this would be less risky and time-consuming. We hope he has learnt from this affair. He likes to be in the swim, but not in real trouble. Dominic is ambitious and his ambitions don't lie in the direction of probation work.

I am fairly easy in my mind about Dominic. What worries me is the effect it may have on the other children. Kathleen is a strong character and I don't see her succumbing to this particular temptation. Her reaction to the affair was to say, affectionately, 'Dominic isn't an addictive type – too hooked on himself.' All that Cuillane had to contribute to the debate was the statement that 'it was not uncommon in the nineteenth century'. She seemed unable or unwilling to narrow the problem down to what was happening in 1964 in her own house. The twins are secretive and prefer to be on their own rather than with friends. We lose them when we go for walks on the Downs and by the sea they have their own part of the beach, which I regularly invade bringing Peg with me. Fergus doesn't like this tendency to be apart, but points out that it doesn't mean they perform satanic rites and are ripe for drug addiction. As for Peg, I don't think she knew what kind of pot we were talking about.

Stephen is the one about whom I am really concerned. He views all people with a delighted interest which can only too easily be interpreted as a particular affection and I have noticed that other children are drawn to him. Even characters as different as my mother and Harpo lay claim to sharing a special understanding with Stephen. In addition to this disarming show of interest, he is fun to be with. He has his father's humour and there is always laughter in the house when they are together. But, and no doubt I lay too much emphasis on this oft-repeated but, he lacks Fergus's toughness of mind. He is an obliging person. I am not saying he would be easily led into doing something that was against his nature; the trouble is, I am not sure what his nature is. I fear that in him curiosity may be stronger than the tendency to formulate principles. In short, I'm not sure how sound is his judgement. During this business with Dominic he went into orbit and we were daily presented with the Stephen who is a stranger to the planet and doesn't understand its life forms.

Heigh-ho. Friends cast even more doubtful glances at Fergus's laboratory, though I think it is really the playing of classical music they are anxious to discourage.

Let us know who to expect at half-term.

Love from one failed parent to another,

Constance

Sussex
April, 1965

My dear Sheila,

I am trying to be delighted for you. Once the divorce was through I knew that you would want to make more changes in your life. It is splendid that you have a senior English post; but why in the depths of Gloucestershire? And will you really enjoy teaching at what sounds ominously like a school for young ladies? I console myself by imagining you looking from the window of one of those lovely stone cottages overhung with wistaria while you wait for the inspiration for the next line of a poem. You are going to address yourself to your poetry now, I hope; otherwise I see no advantage in this rural retreat.

Linnie seems happy at the Guildhall School of Music. I know you think that music doesn't offer much of a life to those who lack great talent; but she seems to get so much joy out of it that I wonder whether sometimes it might not be worthwhile being second-rate. She is such an accepting, undemanding person and will take what comes her way and be thankful. I hope you are not moving away too abruptly at a time when she may be beginning gently to separate from you.

Toby will be well looked after by your parents; but are you

right in thinking that the only hope of reconciliation is for you to be at some distance from him?

Don't move too far away from us all.

Love and misgivings,
Constance

My dear Sheila,

I am sorry, I am sorry, I am sorry! I will cover two sheets with sorriness if you will forgive me.

I was profoundly moved by your comment that you have come to realise you must now take on yourself the role of the partner. As I reflected on this I realised how much I rely on Fergus to supplement and balance my personality. How does one manage without the seemingly unfruitful arguments after which one is surprised to find one's opinions ever so slightly amended; the long talks in bed which over a period of time lead, if not to the solving of problems, then to some sort of accommodation; the acceptance of weakness, the recognition of strength, the ability to laugh at fears and to put anger to one side? You say it's like developing another part of the brain when one part ceases to function. I hope that Gloucestershire may bring you the peace you need to make some sort of sense of this.

I have problems, too. Would I had your courage.

Now that the children are all at school I have time to make discoveries about myself – such as, that I am not good company. I thought of taking a part-time job (goodness knows we could do with the money), but all I have to offer is myself and this doesn't seem to be enough – skills are required. I told Fergus, 'I need worthwhile activities with which to occupy myself.' He, as well as his paid work, has worthwhile activities, which doesn't seem quite fair. Some time ago his priest asked him to visit one of the Roman Catholics in the town prison. This soon led to his visiting several Roman Catholics, with the result that he sees rather less of me. I asked whether there was any reason why I shouldn't do prison visiting. I will not bore you with details, merely say that eventually the powers that be decided that there were several reasons, none of which they were prepared to divulge, why I would not make a suitable prison visitor.

Obviously my capabilities as an adult, as distinct from a mother, were in question. I spent some time in the bedroom studying myself in the long mirror. In my youth I was reckoned to have dress sense and more than a touch of glamour. I had thought to have retained both attributes and I have always indulged the youthful habit of flinging on my clothes in the belief that the effect will not have changed materially down the years. Now, studying myself carefully, I saw a woman with strawlike hair badly in need of a good cut and a figure which no trimming would help. Why did nobody tell me my stomach had spread? I had no idea what this unkempt stranger was good for, if anything. For a week I felt burnt out and useless and produced meals to prove it.

At the weekend Fergus's Jesuit friend stayed with us. I told him I was reading Von Hügel, which I hoped would please him as he isn't impressed with my intellectual powers. He said that if I found Von Hügel congenial, I might try Caussade. When he had left, I asked Fergus if he had anything by Caussade and he produced yet another volume of letters. The Jesuit was right. Von Hügel talks to his niece and I am privileged to overhear. Caussade speaks directly to me. There is a rumour abroad that he died in 1751, but it's not true. He sits across the room from me and his knowledge of my condition is uncanny. 'I can find no particular sin in your conduct, yet I perceive defects and imperfections which might do you great harm if you did not apply a strong remedy. These are uneasiness, foolish fears, depression, weariness and a discouragement not quite free of deliberation, or at least not combated with sufficient energy, all of which tend to diminish your inner peace.' No one has ever known me so well or advised so wisely – 'Be very careful not to allow thoughts which would bring about sadness, uneasiness or depression to remain in your mind. Let them alone, without dwelling on them; despise them and let them fall like a stone into the sea.'

I help in the canteen at the prison now, serving tea and coffee and miscounting change. 'I nearly swindled you,' I said to one con yesterday. 'Don't do that, love,' he answerd. 'That's what I'm in for.' It keeps me occupied and provides some sort of service.

Soon Dominic will be leaving home and then it will be Kathleen and the time will come when my beloved clown, Stephen, will go. Pray that I may grow in wisdom, Sheila, as I pray that you may find your way through the dark wood.

My love,
         Constance

Sussex
May, 1965

My dear Sheila,

It was a joy to hear you on the telephone, though the line was so bad I only heard half of what you said. I gathered, however, that you were phoning from a call-box in the village. It's a relief to know that you're within reach of civilisation of some sort. I would have thought you had had your fill of struggle over the last week, but seemingly you're insatiable since you want an account of the house moving activities from the Richmond end.

Spirits were high as we set out from Sussex. My Fergus and your dear brother, Peter, were excited as two schoolboys allowed into the cab of a steam-engine – the difference being that they were to do the driving. Peter talked much of his experience in the desert, though to my recollection he wasn't in the tank corps. As the marines did most of the driving in the Navy, Fergus couldn't respond in kind, but he recounted tales of his early years in the Wicklows where, he would have us believe, his family was the first to discover the wheel. None of which convinced me that either of them was qualified to drive a high-sided vehicle with limited rear view.

Dominic and Kathleen had volunteered to help and I took

them with me in the car – a procedure to which they only consented because it was apparent that if they so much as set foot in the van I should lie down in front of its wheels. Needless to say we arrived long before the van. Kathleen suggested we should start stacking furniture and move it into the hall.

'You will break your father's heart if you lay a finger on any object,' I said. 'He spent most of last night planning this manoeuvre down to the last cup and saucer.'

Dominic said, 'How much did they get for the house?'

'Just over five thousand.'

'They should have got at least seven.'

Kathleen said, 'I can't stand around here,' and went into the garden. I followed her. She had her period and looked heavy-eyed and pale. That lovely chestnut hair is greasy now and she has lost her sprightliness. She moves as if her limbs drag chains. Adolescence is physically and emotionally cruel to her. We poked about in the shrubbery where the rhododendrons were choking the azaleas whose expiring breath was overpowering. 'They'll make it all neat and tidy, the new people. Just like any other garden. There will never be anywhere like this again for children.' So, you see, Sheila, despite her present misery she counts your home among her blessings.

Fergus and Peter arrived half an hour later. No sooner had Fergus assigned to each of us our allotted task than Toby and Linnie arrived. They were insistent they should help. You seemed particularly anxious to know how they were affected by this upheaval, so I will give you my impressions for what they're worth.

Toby rolled up his sleeves and got to work as if he were exorcising ghosts. Whatever happened to the ghosts, the physical effort certainly brought him back to life. As the day wore on he came more and more to resemble the sturdy boy of his early years.

Linnie wandered sadly from room to room, shadowed by me. 'Do you think this is the best way to say goodbye?' I asked. 'We could go out to lunch. They don't really need us.'

'I have to see it happen.'

'Memories are important, though, aren't they?' I made a pretty speech in defence of memory and the need to keep it intact.

She said, and I don't like to repeat this, for my own sake as much as yours, 'Now that I have left home, I shall want to run back here whenever I am sad. If I see it dismantled I will know I can't go back, won't I? It is like death. They say you never really believe a person is dead if you don't see the body.'

We were in the music room; with Miles's furniture gone, there were only the music stands, two upright chairs and your harp. A room looks smaller without its furniture.

It was one of those fickle spring days, lilac blowing about beyond the window, rain on the wind. I'm sure this must have affected Linnie. When one is young one's body is so tormented by atmospheric pressure. Still, for no reason at all, I can weep on an uncertain spring day. No season so accuses one as spring, saying, look at all this promise and account for yourself. I am afraid I wasn't much help to her. She played the harp and I snivelled.

All that time, Toby was dismantling light fittings, taking out curtain rails, unscrewing hooks. Is one allowed to take all the fixtures? Toby took the lot. He seemed determined the house should be stripped of all its possessions.

Dominic was invaluable. He it was who fully understood that whereas the house had many spaces, the van had but the one into which all the furniture must be compressed. He had his hour of glory, standing at the rear of the van in a 'they shall not pass' attitude until all bowed to his authority. A very good job he made of it, with one exception of which you shall hear later.

During the lunch break the sun shone fitfully and Linnie brightened with it. Kathleen is envious because she has a room of her own, which is Kathleen's idea of absolute independence. Kathleen is a great believer in absolutes and I was pleased to hear Linnie say, 'You soon find out you have exchanged one authority for another. It is much harder to bargain with a landlady about the time you come in in the evening. As for playing the violin, that's out of the question. I'm looking for a deaf house-owner with deaf neighbours.'

Fergus and Peter were relaxing in a manner which suggested the work was all but finished. When I pointed out that we were behind schedule thanks to their late arrival, Peter said, 'We'll soon make up any lost time.' Fortunately, Dominic had the bit between his teeth and Fergus could see that if he did not bestir himself his son would take command of the house as well as the van.

'Now, what can Linnie and I do?' I asked Kathleen when the men had returned to their labours.

'You may well ask,' she said crossly. 'Neither of you has lifted a finger so far.'

She had packed all the crockery and kitchen equipment. I hope it arrived intact? It would not have been well received had I insisted on inspecting her efforts. She and Linnie and I began to pack the books. We had nearly finished when we were aware that the sounds of masculine effort which had echoed about the house were now concentrated on the landing. Ill-humour had displaced the cheery camaraderie of the morning. We finished the books and went into the hall intent on a little gentle gloating.

I will recount this episode in detail since it seems from your letter that Peter and Fergus had not thought fit to mention it to you.

Sheila, it was your upright piano! Fortunately, Peter had had the good sense to protect it with dust sheets and cushions as soon as he saw that there might be a little difficulty in negotiating that sharp bend in the stairs leading down from your bedroom. Which was where it was stuck. Not only did it appear to be immovable, it was also impassable. Peter and Toby were trapped above it. Fergus said, 'Sheila and Miles must have discovered this piano when they moved in. The house was undoubtedly constructed around it.'

I shouted at them not to cause any further damage by attempting to move it. (I inspected it later and I swear it is not marked.) Fergus lost his temper and locked himself in the lavatory. Peter and Toby, to whom retreat was not open, sat on the stairs and sulked. Kathleen and Linnie and I crawled about looking under the legs, but this only confirmed that it was firmly wedged. Eventually, after much mutual recrimination, we agreed to get the remaining furniture and packing cases into the van and then have another think about the piano. Toby and Peter went up to your bedroom to see whether it was possible for them to get out of the window.

While we were putting the last of the cases into the van, and Toby and Peter were convincing themselves that a long ladder was their only hope of escape, the incoming furniture van arrived. Harrods. Sheila, if you could have seen those two benign, rubicund men immaculate in green baize aprons! Had they pattered round their van singing, 'Heigh-ho, heigh-ho, it's off to work we go', it would not have seemed inappropriate. They listened gravely to our tale of woe, too polite to permit even a twinkle of the eye. Then they went into the house to inspect the piano. One of them said to Peter, 'I think it will go back up if you could just ease your end a couple of inches, Sir.' Surprisingly, it did prove possible to move the piano back to your bedroom. While we were congratulating ourselves on the release of Peter and Toby, the Harrods men delicately lofted the piano and conveyed it sedately down the stairs and out to the van.

Here, we encountered a problem. No one had thought to inform Dominic of the existence of the piano. So, it was all to do again. I am afraid your furniture came to you packed by courtesy of Harrods at the price of two bottles of beer.

How wise are those legends about people who are told that whatever they do they must not look back. I went back for one last look from your landing window. 'I will never again see the river from here,' I told myself, as though that view had a magic nowhere else to be found in the whole length and breadth of the river. The sun was out. Best it had not been and I unable to distinguish one grey area from another. But the sun was out and there were willows in the intervening gardens and then that distant flash of blue water. And I remembered walks along the towpath with Daddy on a Sunday afternoon, the pussy willows and catkins, Syon House composed and confident beyond its green lawns, the spume of trees which hides The London Apprentice from view. I remembered you and me at Kew, shouting for Cambridge as the crews toiled past; I remembered walking to Strawberry Hill during my lunch hour in Twickenham and watching fighter planes like gleaming toys in the sky. Why is it that so much of our life is spent longing for drama, and when it does come our way we find that it is the small, unimportant things which we really cherish? Is this what is meant by the sacrament of the present moment? Before I could develop this enquiry – always supposing myself to be able – Linnie joined me.

She said, as if taking up an interrupted conversation, 'So do you think I'm silly to go on with my music?'

'I'd be disappointed if you didn't go on with it.'

'I'm only moderate, you know.'

'Even so, it means a lot to you, doesn't it? What will you do when you leave college – teach?'

She nodded. She looked attractive with sunlight gentle on her dark hair and honey-coloured skin. Not that she will ever be a beauty; there is that in her manner of presenting herself which suggests beauty would be a presumption, an error of taste. But she will lose nothing by seeming to undervalue herself. Some man will feel he has made a great discovery in her. I found myself thinking that she wouldn't need to worry too much about what she did with her music, marriage would claim her energies soon enough. Then I reminded myself that times are changing. To Linnie, marriage, a home and family may not represent the ultimate prize, may not seem desirable. She may even prefer to remain undiscovered.

'Carry on with your music,' I said. 'It will always give you joy so long as you don't hope for too much from it.'

'I don't think I could hope for anything ever again,' she said.

I found that little touch of drama – and who better than me to recognise drama – quite comforting. When grief is on parade it ceases to have the force of a private devotion. Don't you agree?

'You won't find hope so easy to get rid of, my treasure,' I assured her, brisk and nannyish. This ended our conversation, as she likes to be taken seriously. We joined the others. She made a show of greeting Kathleen as if they had been separated for a month rather than ten minutes.

When Fergus and Peter finally drove off, Toby insisted we went to tea at the Copper Kettle. He and Dominic were getting on well. Kathleen and Linnie talked about London life. Kathleen was undiscriminating in her enthusiasm, as willing to embrace the petty restrictions imposed by landladies as the greater freedom of association, as eager for the depravities of Soho as the chic of Shepherd Market, as delighted by the prospect of having money of her own as the necessity to live on cheese when the grant ran out. London was a pageant laid on for her benefit, a twenty-four-hour show so varied its power to stimulate would never fail.

Dominic, when not urging more crumpets on us, was looking beyond his law degree to the time when he would be in chambers. He has been in training for this for a long time and from his manner one might imagine that he had already taken silk. I was impressed by how adult he has become. His broad face and thick dark hair give him an expansive, even luxurious air and this, combined with heaviness of feature and thickness of body, deceptively suggests maturity and a degree of good living for which I can take no credit. He is fashioned thus. It is inconceivable he will not eventually be addressed as M'Lud.

Toby, you will be pleased to know, was by no means daunted. He is quite a big lad now, isn't he? with no padding to disguise bone and sinew. He seemed restless, not so much in his mind as within his skin; as if, after a period of lethargy, he had become conscious of a need for exercise. On an impulse, I asked, 'Does your school send boys on Outward Bound courses?' He was dismissive – too much emphasis on character building. He thought he would like to go to some place where they hadn't yet discovered character. It struck me that he was the one person in this group who had suffered no nostalgia as a result of the day's work. If it is possible physically to pick up one's troubles and dump them, then he seemed to have done it.

There you have my removal story. I look forward to our working holiday with you in August. Judging from your description of the condition of the cottage, the Byrnes will be camping in your garden at intervals throughout the next few years.

Love from us all and don't try to do too much on your own,

Constance

Sussex
June, 1966

My dear Sheila,

You will be surprised to learn that I am going to disagree with you. Can this be Constance, you wonder, biddable, acquiescent Constance, seldom known to be contrary? I must mark these wise words, you will tell yourself as you read.

It is true that during the years you spent with Miles you were cut off from the outside world and you lost most of your friends, apart from Harpo and myself. I concede that there was no one outside your immediate family with whom you had regular contact. Now, consider: when you married, you were twenty-four, had been to Cambridge and served in the WRNS; your ability to socialise was not in doubt in those early years, nor, more important, was your capacity for friendship. I will allow that your social skills may be rusty and that the years with Miles have left you wary and prone to withdraw from close contact; but these problems will right themselves given time and favourable conditions.

It is obvious that the conditions are far from favourable. This school would have been regarded as old-fashioned in its outlook in the thirties. The Headmistress bemoans the fact that while before the war she was regarded as upper class she now finds herself categorised as middle class, a relegation she sees as symptomatic of the decay of the nation. The staff complain, 'We have to teach children of tradespeople now; the butcher's daughter is in the third form.' They are insecure; they see their world under threat, themselves the last defence against barbarism. You would never have been able to work among such people.

For years you have been pushing yourself in the belief that you are indestructible. When you were at your lowest ebb, you decided to take up the challenge of teaching. As if that were not challenge enough, you moved to Gloucestershire, away from your children, your parents and ever further from your devoted Constance. There, not content with one house near enough the river to be a prey to its moods, you bought a stone cottage steeped in the damp of centuries on which we shall all have to work like navvies for the next two years at least. Then, good Labour supporter that you are, you take a post at a school which looks back to a golden era of Edwardian comfort and privilege.

You have made mistakes, but you didn't imagine that once free of Miles you would go through life without making mistakes? A few mistakes here and there don't add up to 'an inadequate personality unable to establish good personal relationships or to handle work situations'.

What you need is rest. The day term ends, pack your bags and head for Sussex, sanity and sanitation. We shall be going to Ireland on 15th August. I can't ask you to join us as my father-in-law is not well, but you are welcome to use our house while we are away. Dominic, Kathleen and Cuillane will be in and out, and Harpo will be there keeping some sort of order and subverting their political judgement.

Please, please be kind to yourself.

My love,
    Constance

Sussex
October, 1966

My dear Sheila,

    I loved the poem you sent me. Beyond my window-pane the grass is dusted with frost, patterned with the red of fallen leaves. The hills are damson against a steely sky. And does my heart sing praise? No, I think only of early darkness penning in reluctant children; mud everywhere and arguments over the cleaning of boots; the battle to keep the house warm with so many males around who never shut a door, and shopping expeditions on icy roads. You, whose situation is so much worse, make a gift of each day, each season.

I am glad you feel better, though I have to tell you that our adviser on matters psychological, Harpo, is not entirely convinced. Are you right in saying you must do three years at this wretched school in order to have some experience to put on paper? Whatever you do, don't let it make you ill.

Linnie seemed well, I thought; and you must have been pleased at the improvement in Toby. I wish I could write as hopefully of Fergus's father. To our great surprise, Dominic gave up a sailing holiday in order to visit him. Kathleen and Cuillane plan to go over at half-term. He will be so pleased to see them. He lies in bed looking more than ever like one of those Old Testament characters who begat many sons. His daughter-in-law had news for him. I have decided to become a Catholic. It was his reaction which convinced me he was terminally ill – he was delighted. His son is still at the fractious stage of life and suspects there is no reason for conversion other than the need to demonstrate yet again a talent for mistiming life; having stood out during the children's younger years, thus causing dislocation, if not friction, now, when it doesn't matter so much (is that theologically sound?) I decide to partake of the feast.

I said to him, 'Wouldn't it be nice if we could share one profound experience?'

He said he had often wished for this and thought it typical of me to dictate the event.

His mother says he is anxious about the instruction, since it was such a disaster last time, and he is afraid of the effect on the children should it fail again. But it won't fail. I have come to believe that, for all its imperfections, the Catholic Church is the custodian of the treasures I hold dear. The priest is a plump, elderly man, benign and unillusioned. I doubt that he rates my chances of being a good Catholic very high, but Catholics are accepting of weakness and I expect I shall be better off failing with them than keeping my chin above water with the Protestants.

My mother is deeply shocked but says, 'Of course, it was inevitable given your circumstances', which is not fair to Fergus who has never put any pressure on me. I hope you and your parents will understand. It has often seemed to me that there is some common ground, which I can't identify, between Methodists and Catholics.

We will try to get down at half-term and lend a hand with the plastering. I am glad the farmer who owns your land is being helpful about the proposed covered way to the loo. Is he the man I met last year – not uncouth nor yet couth, a working farmer? He looked as if he would be effective. Let's hope he can summon up labour to get the work done quickly. I can't bear to think of you trudging out at night in the snow as you did last year. It is a wonder 'flu did not turn to pneumonia.

My love,
Constance

My dear Sheila,

Yours was such an understanding letter. We are so sorry that you did not meet Fergus's father. What sparks would have been struck from that encounter! Fergus is writing to you. He grieves that he saw so little of his father when the chance was there. It was my fault. There were years when we didn't go to Ireland because of trivial household matters I can scarcely bear to think of. My priest is a great comfort and tells me I mustn't take the blame for everything but allow others to have their share; so I am resolved to banish retrospective guilt. Of present guilt there is enough.

Sheila, it seems I have trespassed against Harpo. She is in love with one of those sensitive men who are totally absorbed in the

132

integrity of their own feelings. He owns a second-hand book-shop. Harpo says he is too individualistic to work with other people and, moreover, he would never survive in one of the professions because he doesn't believe in competition. He came for Christmas. Harpo cherishes him, but he will never marry her or anyone else. He is the kind who will drift from one loving woman to another, wasting them all.

Before they arrived, I expressed the hope that they would not discuss the threat to the cosmos. This concern with the cosmos has altered Harpo sadly. She now wears her hair Shetland-pony style and from being one of the most smiling of people, seriousness has settled on her features and weighed them down. She has become worthy. She makes pronouncements instead of conversation. Her clothes have been adapted to suit the new Harpo. Gone the bright colours which, though they did not always flatter her, gave one the sense that she was trying in a very positive way; now she is all rumpled in greys and browns and there is a definite impression that the clothes are telling you she doesn't give a damn for you or your values. When I remarked on this to Kathleen, she said, 'If Aunt Sheila were to turn up in sackcloth you would proclaim it the height of fashion.' (I wouldn't rely on that, Sheila.)

Kathleen then said to me, 'You must be nice to Harpo this Christmas.'

I pointed out that I had been being nice to Harpo for years before Kathleen was born. Imagine my surprise when I was informed, 'You are a proper Martha with Harpo. Whenever she tries to tell you anything about her work, her friends, something interesting that has happened to her, you busy yourself about the house. If it was Aunt Sheila, you would be Mary, sitting at her feet, all attention.'

Even Cuillane was against me. 'It's because she's not married,' she explained gently. 'You wouldn't speak to her the way you do if she had a husband in tow.'

'How do I speak to her?'

'Tolerant, a bit irritated sometimes.'

'She is irritating. I am very forbearing.'

'You rate yourself above her and below Aunt Sheila,' Kathleen said. 'These ratings are formed when people are quite young and they seldom change.'

'I'm sure I never spoke to my mother like that.'

'But your generation wasn't very aware of the patterns of social behaviour.'

'We were far more socially conscious, believe me.'

'I don't mean the never filling a teacup to the brim, or tongs with the sugar and using a butter knife. I mean what is actually going on between people. People in groups compete to establish dominance.'

Stephen said, 'Thus spake Cathleen ni Houlihan.'

'Don't interfere in things you are too young to understand, little brother.'

'She with the fire in her eyes . . .'

I said, 'I want you both in the kitchen, please.'

'When you're losing an argument you always resort to the kitchen,' Kathleen said.

'Are you winning then, Kathleen?' Stephen chanted. 'Is it winning you are?'

She pushed him into the hall where they wrestled, suddenly serious, faces devoid of expression, like chess players contemplating which piece to annihilate. I hate to see this grim application to violence.

'Where do you get these ideas from?' I asked Kathleen when I had her installed at the sink. She shrugged her shoulders, her mind now occupied with getting the washing up done so that she could go out with her friend Stella. She has been reading Doris Lessing recently; I suppose that may be the answer.

I find this all rather distressing. Friendship is something I value. Whatever else I am, I am a good, cherishing friend. It may be that I expect things from Harpo that I wouldn't expect of my married friends. I admit that I put myself out for them in a way I don't for her. But this is natural, surely? One person can be absorbed into the family in a way that two cannot. Harpo should regard it as a mark of intimacy and a privilege that I don't fuss over her. When she arrived I said to her, 'My children tell me

I'm getting bossy and not considerate of my friends' feelings. How do you find me?'

She grinned and said, 'Bossy and not considerate of my feelings, of course.' She added, without rancour, 'Well, it's your home and you are very much in charge. I appreciate that.'

This is not how I see myself. I see myself as tolerant, open-handed, relaxed, welcoming, accepting of all comers, of whom there are many in and out of this house. I have a few house rules, yes, and I don't like anyone to get under my feet when I'm working, and I have my own way of doing things and. . . . Am I very much in charge, Sheila? Formidably so? I am so fond of Harpo. I hope I haven't made her feel I don't value her.

I resolved I would bite out my tongue rather than say one unkind word about this ghastly Hugh. In the event, it proved possible to be pleasant to the man. He is tall and thin with crinkly pale gold hair, a long delicate face, vague blue eyes, a weak mouth and a general appearance of fragility. But not the kind whose principles prevent his accepting hospitality. He wined and dined well without being greedy and squared up to long walks on the Downs. He was good with the children. It was easy to see where the charm lay. He fits in and makes an amiable, undemanding companion; there will always be a place for him by someone's fireside.

Let me know about your Christmas and tell me – are all children as critical of their parents as mine are of me?

Love,

Constance

Sussex
March, 1967

My dear Sheila,

It was such a surprise to hear your voice on the telephone that I fear I didn't respond adequately. You were uncharacteristically incoherent. Something is wrong, isn't it? You have been angry about the school for a long time, but this was more than anger.

I was left with a jumble of impressions which I later arranged into what may be an erroneous sequence of events. Are you telling me that the Headmistress colluded with the master of the local hunt in an attack on a bunch of hippies who had had the temerity to camp on a field near the school and that you were witness to the scattering of the campers and the mangling of two of their dogs? I'm not clear whether the field is owned by the school or whether it was sufficiently close to the school grounds for the hippy goings-on to represent a moral danger to the pupils (or merely an affront to the Headmistress's sensibilities).

Fergus and I had an argument about this. I maintained that the question of ownership was important and he said this was an attitude all too typical of a property-owning culture. To hear him talk one would think he was born in a field and educated in a hedge school.

Whatever the rights and wrongs of the case, it has obviously greatly upset you. I wanted to ring you back, but couldn't find the telephone number of your friend in the village. When I did find it, you had returned home. Your friend sounded troubled about you. 'She's not used to country ways,' she said gently, as if the beating up of unauthorised campers were a time-honoured rural ritual. 'People feel very strongly about the land. But it was dreadful that the dogs were savaged – and, of course, she saw it happen.' I suspect you have a sympathiser there but not an ally.

Let me know how you're feeling now. Another, less incoherent, telephone call would be very welcome.

My love,
Constance

P.S. Fergus says you have only to say the word and he will set camp on the lawn of the master of the hunt.

My dear Sheila,

Reports of strange goings-on in Gloucestershire are reaching me.

First, you tell me that the battle of the hippies is still being waged. I must admit to finding it a rather alarming phenomenon and I can understand that, pathetic or otherwise, local people have the feeling the country is drifting towards anarchy. You say the hippy kind of loose living is nothing to compare with what goes on within the stone walls of many a picturesque farm cottage. I must bow to your superior knowledge.

Now, in today's post, comes a distressed letter from Linnie telling me that you offered yourself as a witness when the case went before the magistrates, the Chairman of the Bench also being Chairman of the Governors. She enclosed a cutting from the local paper which suggests that you made some rather wild statements and subsequently attempted to interrupt the proceedings of the court. Fortunately, the fact that you misappropriated the John of Gaunt speech from *Richard II* convinced the beaks that you were not responsible for your actions. Can it really be true that you were hustled out of court shouting, 'This fortress built by gentry to ensure/Though wits be feeble privilege prevails . . .'?

I long to hear your version of events and to know the outcome – did you get your resignation in before you were sacked?

      Love from your law-abiding Constance and unstinted
         admiration from Fergus

My dear Sheila,

I had no idea, so confused was poor Linnie's letter, that you were really ill. You say you knew at the time that it was a kind of madness, but had not recognised it as madness itself. A purifying madness. The fact that it was followed by a complete collapse – whereas you had expected to feel free as never before – does nothing to detract from its efficacy. Would anything less have convinced you that you cannot carry on at that school? You have not lost your way, my love; you are finding it with every leaden minute that passes.

Don't fret Linnie. Let her nurse you. I think you are mistaken in thinking that she is glad of a pretext for being unemployed; she worked hard at the Guildhall and it won't hurt her to have a break before she looks for work. It's good for her to have this opportunity to show her love for you. Cherish the time with her.

I will try to come down soon. In the meantime, we all send our love to you and Linnie,

   Constance

           Sussex
          June, 1967

My poor darling,

It was heart-breaking to see you so frail, face all eyes and bone and hair snowy. You say the flakes have been falling for years, but I never noticed a single one. No matter. You have a strong thatch, this whiteness will be becoming once you are well again.

I have been thinking about you so much since I returned. You, usually so quick to the point, to fear company because you get left behind when words come from all corners of the room; you, to whom disputation was a delight, to lie in bed vainly trying to reconstruct conversations so as to arrive at the meaning, upset when you don't agree with an opinion, the overworked brain stuffed with cotton wool. These are dark times, indeed.

Rest, close your ears to conversation, ask no question of your brain, forget the time, the day, the place. Watch the clouds move across the window. The mind will heal slowly.

You will be in my thoughts and prayers day and night.

  Love,
    Constance

My dear Sheila,

You plead for news because you are tired of lying in bed with nothing to do except watch the clouds drifting across the sky. I had thought quiet would be good for you; but since you ask, the Byrnes' lives are not short of incident.

Dominic, my first-born, who at one time my mother thought might well become a priest, is living in sin in a rented room in the seamier part of Holland Park. My mother says he may still become a priest, but I would rather he made an honest woman of the girl, Angela. I am so far gone in middle-class morality that I am not prepared to have them sleep together in our house. I explained this to them in a civilised way – separate bedrooms or the nine-thirty back to London. Fergus, rather to my surprise, didn't say, 'Your mother feels . . .' but 'We feel . . .' I was so grateful to him I didn't attend to what it was he actually told them about our feelings, but he must have put it quite well because they stayed, in separate bedrooms, and during the day wandered off into the countryside to do I care not what. We all got on very well.

In my heart (or whatever region it is where these things are worked out – it doesn't seem to be the brain, in my case) I'm not sure that Dominic is wrong. But it's not my way and I have seven children and can't at my age start to adapt to seven different life styles. The attitudes of the young are no more attractive in a middle-aged woman than long hair and miniskirts. A line has to be drawn somewhere – in this case, outside the spare room with the double bed.

While I was in a state of moral confusion, Angela's mother came down to look us over. She was a haughty, disparaging woman, intimidatingly well dressed in a linen suit the colour of milk chocolate. Displeasure gave her face a slightly bilious hue. She was very much on her guard; but there was something about her, perhaps the need to be on her guard, which my mother would have described as 'not quite'. She looked round our sitting-room, which was at its best, french windows open on to a tangle of honeysuckle, as if each piece of furniture might give cause for offence.

'You have a lot of space here, haven't you?' she said, frowning.

'It doesn't seem like it when all the children are home.'

'Our house is very compact.'

The only children who were at home were Stephen and Cuillane. No human being is completely predictable, and on this of all days my quietest child was in the garden learning to play her brother's drums, while he marched round the lawn doing his impression of Hitler invading the Rhineland.

'What do your neighbours make of this?' she asked.

'They are out for the day. If it irritates you I can tell them to stop.'

She was not prepared to admit to irritation. Instead, she addressed herself to the painting of tinkers in Connemara which hangs over the mantelpiece. 'Times are changing, of course; but this isn't the kind of thing we expected of Angela.' She said this not to invite sympathy or an exchange of confidences, but to let it be known that their expectations were of a special order. When I said I could appreciate her concern, she looked affronted. As we were not to discuss our concerns it was difficult to know how to proceed.

'You used to live in East Molesey, I believe?' I said, with some notion that if you trace a person back to their roots they become explicable, if not likeable. 'I worked in Twickenham. A long time ago, during the war.'

'We moved from there. It wasn't what it was. People built a bungalow on the field next to our house. They had gnomes in the garden.' For the first time she looked me full in the face; it was so important to her to establish that she was a cut above gnomes.

I said, 'How awful', but it wasn't heartfelt enough to make a bond between us. I took to the kitchen and left her with our photograph album. Cuillane and Stephen joined us for tea. I was amused to note that, nonchalantly though they had accepted Dominic's affair, they were embarrassed in front of Angela's mother.

'Though you might not have thought it from that uproar in the garden, Cuillane is the studious one in our family,' I said, sacrificing my child in time of adversity. 'When she goes to university . . .'

'Ah, but she will have to pass her exams before she can do that, won't she?' Angela, we were reminded, was at London University; any talk of university would, therefore, be regarded as territorial infringement. When she felt she had made the position sufficiently clear, she relented enough to ask Cuillane, 'And what are you studying?'

'Classics.'

'We weren't allowed to read anything else when I was at school. Woe betide any girl who was caught with a copy of *The Rosary* or *The Mistress of Shenstone*. What are you reading at the moment?'

'Thucydides.'

She examined the cake on her plate and pushed it to one side. 'I see.' She looked towards the french windows, chin high.

Stephen said, 'I'm going to read history.'

She did not ask him what he was reading at present. She was afraid we would score off her again.

'But what I really want is to be a drummer.'

'I hope you're better than your sister.' It was a response, tart, but definitely a response.

'Come out in the garden and I'll show you.'

Unexpectedly, she accepted his invitation.

'She didn't like me, did she?' Cuillane said. It is seldom she arouses hostility in anyone.

'She thought we were too clever by half.'

'I don't see anything clever in reading Thucydides.'

Every time I see her reading Greek I am astonished by her cleverness, but I can see that to her it is all a matter of set books. 'Do you enjoy it?' I asked.

'Oh yes. It helps one to understand how the European mind was formed.' She got up and went to the window. 'He really is good, isn't he? Do you think he will become a drummer?'

'I hope not. It's such a rackety life.'

'She's loving it. Look at her. She's really loving it.'

As he drummed, her feet stepped to the rhythm. This was not the jigging about of joints by which I acknowledge rhythm; she knew exactly what she was doing with heel, toe, hips.

'My husband and I once won a quickstep competition at the Hammersmith Palais,' she said when she returned to the sitting-room. She smoothed down her immaculate skirt. 'That was a long time ago, of course.' She appended the 'of course' as if it were a rebuke intended to curb whatever thoughts I might have on the matter.

'But you still dance?' I persisted.

'It doesn't do. My husband is in insurance. One of the old-fashioned, reliable City firms. It doesn't expect its senior staff to make an exhibition of themselves. The first company dance we went to, we did the rumba and they cleared the floor for us. People applauded; but we could see it hadn't gone down well at the top table.'

Stephen said, 'I bet you were terrific,' and I said, with a dim idea of giving something in return for this confidence, 'Would you like to see round the house?'

'What a lot of books,' she said in Fergus's study. 'Do you have to dust them all?' She bent down to examine the tattered dust jackets. 'I'd have these off.'

In our bedroom, she said, 'You've got nice wide window-sills. Ours are so narrow I can't keep any pots on them and I do like to have flowers in the room. Of course, I've got a lot of china ones, but it's not the same as the real thing.'

She hesitated on the landing and I thought I knew what was in her mind. 'They don't sleep together while they are here.' I wanted her to know where I stood, in so far as I stood anywhere.

She shrugged her shoulders. 'My husband won't have them in the house.'

We were both floundering. I thought it was time for mutual comfort. I said, 'Let's hope they will be kind to each other.'

She sorted that out crisply. 'So long as they are careful, that's all I ask.'

She looked at her watch. 'I shall have to leave now if I am to catch the five-fifteen. My husband doesn't know I have come here, so I must be back before seven-thirty.'

I offered to walk to the bus stop with her, but she insisted on calling a taxi. I think she wanted to take a formal leave of us. 'Angela likes your house,' she said as she stood in the hall. She seemed to regret this admission and, drawing her personality about her along with her gloves, added, 'She says it's so comfortably shabby.'

What did she mean, shabby? I work hard to ensure that our house does not appear shabby. Each spring I touch up any window frame from which the paint has quite peeled away. Was it the bathroom she had in mind? She had said earlier that their house in Surbiton was beautifully decorated when they moved in. 'We didn't have to do anything, except for the bathroom. It had a white bath. That had to go, of course.' Our bath is white and hugely stained where the taps have dripped and the plug needs expert attention, so that when a guest has a bath either Fergus or I has to fit it securely in place; but it holds water and what else does one ask of a bath? Neither that, nor the ingenious bell-rope Fergus has fitted to the lavatory cistern in place of the broken chain, justifies referring to our house as shabby.

When she had gone, Stephen said, 'She was fun, wasn't she?'

Cuillane was uncharacteristically angry. 'She was a load of old rubbish. We don't want her here again.'

While I was writing this, Linnie's letter arrived. She tells me she is collecting all your poems and plans to type them and send them to a publisher. That is a commendably sensible daughter. I hope you realise your good fortune.

I know you are unable to cope with too many people, so I won't allow you to be invaded by the Byrnes; but I would like to come on my own if this is permitted. I don't want to give Linnie any trouble and should be happy to stay in a b. & b. in Stroud. It is many years since I had any time to myself. My family regard me as being totally domesticated and it would do them no harm to know that I am capable of surviving in the wild.

Love, much, much love, from us all to you and Linnie,
    Constance

Sheila, my dear,

I do so wish we might have recourse to that arrogant, demanding abomination, the telephone. You must cease your membership of the Non-Telephone-TV-User Society. I need to speak to you so that you can hear the warmth and utter conviction with which I assure you that all this self-loathing is a symptom of weakness, just as aching limbs and throbbing head are symptoms of flu.

You are not useless, selfish, a failure; you are ill, Sheila. If proof were needed, your eulogy of me would serve. Mothering and organisational skills: who can this paragon be? Certainly no one my family would recognise. When you make these foolish comparisons, remember that so far as household tasks are concerned, I have a labour force at my disposal. Kathleen and Cuillane do a certain amount of house cleaning, resentfully, as befits young people of fifteen and eighteen respectively. Gillian, at ten, actually likes cooking; which is to be encouraged, being the first sign of independent life in one who has until now been too much under the influence of her twin.

James is a nice lad, but, like Kathleen, more than a mite thrustful. Since it came upon Gillian that the one great art form is to be discovered in the kitchen, he has had to exercise his leadership skills on Stephen. This is not so rewarding as it might seem, because even when Stephen gives the outward appearance of co-operating, one is never entirely sure what is going on within. 'You would make a good spy,' I heard James say last week. 'Except that you would be caught because you are so careless.' James would not make a good spy. It is perhaps a good thing in one who has a strong temper that storm signals should be unmistakably visible so that those in danger can take cover; but, hothead though he may be, he is a robust lad and works well in the garden under supervision, provided it is accepted that the labourer is worthy of his hire.

Peg likes mending. When she was young she cared for her dolls tenderly, unlike Kathleen, who beat hers up. My mother never ceases to point out, 'That one is a real little mother.' Now, dolls discarded, she looks about for animate substitutes. We are all, adults, children, animals, subjected to Peg's mothering. Our long-suffering lurcher is at this moment having his paw bound up. So, you see, even the cherishing is now in the hands of an eight-year-old.

And then there is Fergus, without whom . . . I won't say we haven't had our difficult patches, but they are part of the weathering. He said the other week that he would like to run a pharmacy in a village. 'In Ireland, perhaps. A small town in Ireland.' I have the impression something in him is spent, that if he had not had seven children and a wife to support he might have broken loose and done work more to his liking. Who knows? The fact is, we did marry and have seven children. What we might otherwise have done is not relevant.

What I'm trying to say, as I ramble on, is, 'Don't make the mistake I made with you and Miles.' The Byrnes are not the ideal family. Fergus and I are only together because we have become part of the furniture of each other's life – a bit worn here, a place there that won't bear much weight, some repairs visible, and faded overall, but moulded by our requirements and cherished accordingly.

Think how much we all love you and try to believe you are worth all our care and concern.

Love,

Constance

P.S. I have had a long letter from Toby. Life in the desert is the only life; just as two months ago, there was nothing to compare to the rarefied atmosphere of the high sierra. We shall make a travel writer of the lad yet.

Sussex
October, 1967

My dear Sheila,

Linnie tells me she's been reading my letters to you and will I please produce a new one. The request comes opportunely. A week ago the police arrested the man who lived solitary with his wife at the Manderley house. Apparently, the house was full of stolen objects, a modern treasure horde. The value of its contents increases with the telling; paintings of humble origin are now attributed to Rubens.

Mrs George Raft (her name is really Mrs Shipman), never previously having set foot in any of our houses, was suddenly in one or other of them most of the day, protesting at the wickedness of authority. She says, 'He just liked having nice things. And he looked after them so well. The people they're going back to will never look after that silver the way he did.' One is tempted to have the same feeling of sympathy towards the Shipmans as to an adoptive couple forced to return their charges to the natural parents.

There is obviously a difference in our conception of how life is to be lived. It is possible, of course, that she does not have concepts. I would find it more accurate to describe her as conceptless than innocent. She must be quite young for she is plump without being flabby and dimples come and go in her cheeks without leaving a trace, let alone a furrow. Yet I would never think of her as carefree. She has big china-blue eyes which give an odd impression of not performing the usual functions of observation and I am never sure when she looks at me whether she has me in focus or whether to her I am merely an animated blur. She seems as tenuously related to her surroundings as a baby, yet she evinces none of a baby's delight in daily discovery; of all the emotions those big eyes could register, surprise is the one I would least expect to see.

'Did your husband ever sell any of the paintings?' I asked, not convinced that it was a matter of good stewardship.

'That's what my solicitor keeps saying,' she said resentfully. 'Did I know about the transactions, that's what he says.'

She had been with me an hour on this occasion and I could see I would have to ask her to stay to lunch. It seemed not unreasonable that she should satisfy my curiosity in return. 'And did you know? I mean, did they come and go, your treasures? Did one replace another from time to time?'

'I wouldn't have noticed. One silver teapot is much like

another. As for the paintings – fat women with off-the-shoulder dresses, off the breast sometimes.' She pursed her rosebud mouth in disapproval. 'If you're as fat as that you can't get away with it.'

It seems inconceivable she should be as naïve as she pretends. Yet her sense of grievance is genuine enough.

'We saw so little of you,' I said, trying to introduce a note of reality into our discussion over lunch. 'You never accepted invitations or invited anyone into your house. Why was that?'

'I can't be bothered with entertaining. I'm no cook. And then there was the stuff. You can't trust people with your belongings. Look what's happened to us now.' She put down her coffee cup. 'I'm getting short of cash. How am I supposed to live while all this is going on?'

'Perhaps you could get a job,' I suggested. She left shortly after this, saying she intended to call on the Vicar.

As I washed up I reflected that shameful though it may be, there is no doubt that this episode has brightened the village considerably. No wonder we are all such avid readers of detective stories; the absence of police intervention in our lives is obviously a loss for which we have to find a substitute. At teatime I rang the vicarage.

'Is Mrs Shipman still with you?' I asked the Vicar's wife.

'Oh, goodness! Is she on her way here?'

'She was, about two hours ago.'

'Well, she didn't arrive.'

Now that we were so well into the detective situation, we both recognised the ominous phraseology. The Vicar's wife insisted I should go round to the Shipmans' house to make sure all was well. 'And you must ring me back and reassure me,' she said eagerly.

The door-bell did not seem to work and the knocker was stiff. The letter box had one of those brushes attached which prevents draughts and discourages prying eyes. I walked round the untidy flowerbeds and peered in windows, holding my breath in anticipation. The sitting-room betrayed no sign of occupation, no books or newspapers, not even an ashtray with cigarette ends in it. The kitchen bore witness to Mrs Shipman's statement that she was no cook: neither crockery nor pans had been disturbed. I went home and rang the vicarage. This time I spoke to the Vicar, who sounded exasperated but allowed himself to be persuaded by his wife that he should accompany me in a search for Mrs Shipman.

We walked in the direction of the river. Physically, Mrs Shipman seemed unsuited to downland. As you probably remember, between the village and the river there is a stretch of water meadows intersected by numerous channels. We walked beside a channel overhung with willows. The bank on one side is a foot above the meadow and walking along this ridge we could see the flat, waterlogged fields stretching so far into the distance the river itself was hidden, although we could see people walking dogs along its banks. There were sheep in the near field, cows in the far fields. No sign of Mrs Shipman, upright or horizontal. We called to the dog-walkers but they were too far ahead to hear us. Nothing in their behaviour indicated they had come across anything untoward. The Vicar, neither a walker nor a detective story reader, was getting tetchy.

Half-way across the field I saw a sheep lying on its back. It was so still that at first I thought it was dead; but it must have been gathering strength for further effort, for suddenly it rolled from side to side, its little hooves stabbing the air unavailingly. Then it was still again, legs sticking up like dead twigs. The Vicar and I crossed to it. The poor thing was panting with exertion or fright. The Vicar, reluctantly accepting the role of good shepherd, gingerly eased a boot beneath the backbone while I tugged at the heavy fleece. The sheep made a convulsive effort and righted itself, whereupon it relieved itself mightily.

'Oh dear,' I said. 'I hope it's going to be as simple as that with Mrs Shipman.' The Vicar, his face screwed up in distaste, gazed in the direction of the village, his eyes homing in on the church spire. Until then I had looked upon this as an afternoon's outing not unpleasantly spiced with drama; now the possibility that we might actually find her face down in the river made my legs tremble. But we saw no sign of her, dead or alive. When we returned to the vicarage, the Vicar telephoned the police station in town.

By now I felt upset and guilty. The seriousness of the matter was emphasised by the visit of a police inspector, who told me that it had been very foolish to set out on a search without informing the proper authorities. He asked whether Mrs Shipman had seemed in a distressed state when she left me. I told him she hadn't been exactly happy, but I hadn't felt she was distressed in the way he meant. He thought I was a tiresome, hair-splitting woman.

Peg and the twins had returned from school and were quarrelling in the garden. As the Inspector and I talked, Stephen wheeled his bicycle past the window and propped it against Fergus's shed. After a few words with James he came into the house.

'That poison Dad's brewing smells awful,' he called out.

'My husband has taken to brewing his own beer,' I explained to the Inspector. It is remarkable how lame the truth can sound when someone else has a livelier scenario to hand.

Stephen came into the room and did a guilty start which would have ensured him a part in any Victorian melodrama. The Inspector, a tired, heavy man, was unamused.

'We are a little concerned about Mrs Shipman,' I said to Stephen, endeavouring to signal to him that the Inspector and I were at one and that he was to co-operate with us. 'Did you by any chance see her on your way home?'

The Inspector said, 'I would prefer to ask the questions, if you don't mind, Ma'am.'

Silence ensued. It gave the Inspector time to observe Stephen. You know how it is with Stephen; he has something of Fergus in him and finds strict adherence to factual truth dull. When he tells me what has happened at school I have difficulty in distinguishing between what I am expected to believe and what is offered for my enjoyment. This, of course, does not justify his telling the inspector that he had seen Mrs Shipman riding pillion on PC Barker's motor scooter. Stephen's blond hair and angular features give him a Saxon look which arouses expectations of straightforward reliability. People get muddled about him. I could see the Inspector was muddled, confronted by a youth who promised to deal straight and turned out to be the joker in the pack.

The Inspector said, 'Don't get clever with me, lad. Did you or did you not see Mrs Shipman on your way home?'

Stephen appeared to consider and then asked, with every appearance of craftiness, 'Why do you want her?'

The Inspector's neck went red but he answered with commendable restraint, 'I want her because your mother has reported her missing.'

Stephen said to me, 'That wasn't very sporting of you.'

'He hasn't seen her,' I said hastily. 'He's at the age when they have to tease.'

'I've got two of my own.' But I could see that hadn't reconciled him to this particular one. It is a bad policy to get on the wrong side of the police, so I persuaded him to have a cup of tea. Stephen went up to his room to contemplate the sad fact that there is a Judas in every person, even one's own mother.

As the Inspector was leaving, Fergus arrived home from a trip to Reading. When we told him what had happened, he said he had seen Mrs Shipman at the station, waiting for the London train.

'Perhaps she has gone to see her solicitor,' I suggested.

'Gone back on the game, more like,' the Inspector said sourly.

I blame myself for not offering to lend her something from the housekeeping to tide her over.

There it is, our little drama. What do you make of it? It says much for Mrs Shipman's persuasive powers that we prefer to think of her as a victim, the more so now that we know to what lengths she has been driven by her misfortunes. I hear that the Vicar prayed for her at Matins last Sunday. Several ladies of the parish plan to contact the Salvation Army in the hope that they may gain information on her whereabouts. Kathleen is considering the probation service as a future career.

I hope you feel well enough to stay with your parents in

Ealing for Christmas. It is no use suggesting a visit here, too noisy and overpopulated. I will try to come to you for a few days at the beginning of December.

I am to be received into the Catholic Church next Sunday. Pray for me.

We all send our love to you and Linnie,
Constance

Sussex
December, 1967

My dear Sheila,

What a splendid Christmas present for you. You say you cannot cope with it, but your part is done. The publishers will take care of the printing, and if you don't feel able to do the proof-reading, Linnie will do it for you.

Let it lie in your mind, my love, and you will gradually see what a blessing this is; a new life springing from the darkness. We are all so delighted and send our love to you and Linnie and your parents.

Constance

Sussex
April, 1968

My dear Sheila,

I am up at six o'clock to write this letter. The magnolia outside the front door is a mass of blossom, its laden skirts sweeping the lawn. Beyond, the trunks of silver birches shine in a white mist; the other trees are as yet only lightly sketched on the day. The grass is combed with silver. There are primroses and primula between the cracks in the paving stones. I must do this daily. It will refresh my soul and sweeten my nature.

You did even better, walking while the earth was still steaming. I like to visualise you and Linnie on the heath – an old crone and a young girl, you say – but I'll have none of that; I see the mist parting to reveal two timeless figures walking slowly side by side. You are not to imagine yourself as woebegone as Tess.

151

Your sense of timing is much sharper; had you stabbed the dastardly Alec D'Urberville it would have been long before Chapter 56.

I can understand that Linnie found it frightening, some people have this horror of great space; but you must embrace it, if you feel that its vast disinterestedness is healing. Don't let other people's fears drive you back into that cottage where the walls close in on you. I am not so sure about the lone nocturnal walks and should be happier had you a dog.

Let me have news of the progress of the book.

Love,

Constance

Sussex
August, 1968

My long lost friend,

It was good to have news direct from your pen again, even though Linnie had faithfully informed us of your progress. Your spectacular progress, it would seem. You draw a vivid picture of these publishing folk. It must be exciting for you; the first stimulating contacts you have made since the days when you handled Miles's affairs. But isn't this all happening rather fast? Even allowing for your phenomenal powers of recovery, time is needed for proper healing.

I was sorry you weren't able to come to us during the summer, but perhaps it was as well since we are not at our best just now. Kathleen has set her face against university, which she dismisses as élitist. Fergus pointed out that it would continue to be an élitist education if people like her turned their backs on it; but to no avail. She is taking a social science course at the technical college. We are lectured daily on the evils of the class system and the baleful influence of the family. She is at an age where to shock is as necessary as scratching an itch.

We are taking her and Cuillane out to supper tonight before going to the local theatre. This will involve arguments about dress. Cuillane, in her absurd miniskirt, is like some shy plant peeled of its early foliage; while Kathleen's long hair does service for a skirt. Fergus says he doesn't care to be seen with them and I say, to give myself courage, 'Not only will you be seen with them, but you will be seen to be enjoying yourself.' All will be well. As soon as we arrive at the restaurant and encounter the first disapproving glance, Fergus will behave as if he was escorting two princesses.

I tremble for them. They are both innocent of the effect they have on males. It sometimes seems to me that our generation, which put on war-paint and then went off to dances in our chaste navy and white, had a far better idea what we were about than they have.

I tremble about many things lately and tears come all too readily. Kathleen says it is the time of life. 'Women who don't have hot flushes have a worse time emotionally.'

Enough of this domestic trivia. When are we to see this book of poetry for which, to quote that blurb, 'women have been waiting'? Doesn't that rather narrow the appeal, or is it that women are the buyers of poetry?

My love – and take things easy if you know how to –
Constance

Sussex
September, 1968

Sheila,

Years ago I wrote to you suggesting we had a holiday together before we became encumbered with children. But the children came fast as snowflakes and we said, 'It will have to be when they are older and can be left in the care of husbands.'

Last night I had a dream. I seemed to be in the WRNS and involved in some kind of marathon. I panted along, protesting that I hadn't meant to get caught up in this; but as I looked around me the procession filled the picture. As far as the eye could see there were bobbing heads and moving limbs. There was no way out, no quiet place in the distance, just a mass of people running and me running with them. I realised this had been all I had known of life and I wanted to step outside it.

Sheila, let's have that holiday in East Anglia and walk together along the lonely pebble beach. Will you, can you?'

Constance

My dear Sheila,

Yes, I understood that you couldn't get away.

What interesting people you are meeting. And how very generous of John Betjeman. That will be a great help to you. Alarming, though, this expectation of a firework display whenever you appear in public.

I am sorry we are unable to come to the launching party, but, as I think Harpo told you, my mother is very ill. We would have liked her to be here, but the house is too noisy and, in any case, she needs expert nursing. Dominic would be delighted to represent the Byrnes, if this is possible? He now has a Spanish girlfriend of great charm and irreproachable morals.

We look forward to receiving the promised copy and shall immediately besiege the local bookshops.

Our love and good wishes,

Constance

Sussex
January, 1969

My dear Sheila,

This should have been written sooner, but my mother's death has set me back. Your letter was a comfort because you probably understand better than anyone else that ours was not a warm relationship. As you say, she was gallant during her long widowhood and probably got far more enjoyment from my children than from the result of her own child-bearing. Of course I didn't expect you to come to the funeral. That radio interview was of paramount importance.

The poetry was a surprise. I had not realised how meticulously you had chronicled the 'days, months, years which are the rags of time'. Some lines plumb depths of despair, yet almost immediately you turn aside, unwilling to prolong pain or joy. You are a sharp observer of the human scene, merciless, one might say.

I'm glad Linnie has this job in the music library, particularly as it will enable her to continue with her orchestral work.

My love to you both,

Constance

Sussex
February, 1969

My dear Sheila,

Yes, I would like to come in April. Fergus will take care of things here. Then he is to have a holiday on his own in Ireland. He is not happy in his work and needs time to think about the future; though with so many children still to educate, I don't know what options are open to him. He dislikes the man under whom he now works, but, murder apart, what can one do about that?

All sounds a bit wooden, will do better when we meet.

My love,

Constance

Sussex
May, 1969

Sheila –

That was a wonderful time you gave me. This success, so well deserved, has transformed you. All the potential which Miles inhibited has been realised and, as happens when one is happy and rewarded, the gifts flow out to others.

The cottage looked lovely. It must be the best time to see it, with the blossom out and the daffodils. You're wise to stay there, though I wish you had a more congenial neighbour than your dour farmer, useful though he is as a supplier of eggs.

In haste to catch the post,

Love,

Constance

Sussex
May, 1969

My dear Sheila,

Drat Harpo, the woman talks too much. Yes, I did return home to find a letter from Miles waiting and I have destroyed it; but since you insist you have a right to know the contents, I have little difficulty in remembering.

The publication of your book proved that poetry was what you had always cared about; the driving force in your life was the need to write and he had come a poor second. That is why he had to leave you. There was always something which you withheld from him. As he read the poems he saw that you had used him; he saw himself in every line, even the poems inspired by your school experiences foreshadowed his advent. He must have it that you did not care about him, yet he insists that you are as obsessed with him as he still is with you.

I have confidence, having seen you so recently, that you will be able to put this out of your mind. You are well rid of him.

Fergus goes away next week. I can see he is aching for the moment when he can shut the door on us all. I should have realised long ago that he had this need to be on his own for a time.

I must get down to some housework now.

My love,

Constance

P.S. Dominic is to marry Manuela in September. My mother left him the house in Ealing, so they will at least have a roof over their heads. Not fair on the other children. Fortunately Kathleen and James, who care most about fairness, are not interested in property.

My dear Sheila,

Some of my recent letters have sounded stilted? Am I holding something back, you ask. Would that I had something to hold back. The truth is I have begun to fear you may find me rather dull. I am an unconfident person, with small talents. If, just for a time, someone's attention seems to wander, I am like an actress who has made the mistake of looking at the audience and has seen someone yawn. You have told me so much about the people you are meeting – a host of new characters introduced at a time when the action begins to flag. I can't respond in kind. My concerns are with my children and domestic life. Even the characters at my disposal are giving me trouble.

I have a growing fear that Kathleen may become a nun. She has lately developed a certain gravity – not intensity, or anything tiresome, but some profound concern with the spiritual life. I dare not mention it to Fergus for fear that once out in the open the idea will be like a demon released from a box. I look at her when I think she won't notice, I hardly dare breathe on her. It would be wrong for her, I know it would; but if I gave a hint of how I felt it might kindle something in her. I would sacrifice all my other children – except Stephen – to prevent this. I feel quite pagan, constantly offering them up; take them, Lord, take them, be assuaged.

Fergus seems better for his time in Ireland; but whether it has settled anything or not, I don't know. We are off to Spain for this wedding at the beginning of September. There! I shall have something different to write about, new place, new people.

My love,
Constance

Sheila,

For a full account of the wedding you must apply to Fergus,
or to Kathleen, the representative sibling. I don't recall a great
deal about it – so much wine in all that heat. Fergus and
Manuela's parents made a good job of conversing in Latin while
I grimaced and made signs. Dominic made a speech in Spanish
– considerably shorter than it would otherwise have been.
Manuela looked not the least daunted at the prospect of making
her home in our grey little land.

We leave in three days. How fleeting is joy! Time has got
clogged with dust here, the heat slows the pace of life. This is
the land of *mañana* – Ireland, too. I prefer it. Somewhere
inside this brisk, busy woman I have discovered a lotus-eater.

I like it all. I like the distinctive smell of the place, compounded of heat and drains, garlic and oil and strong tobacco. I
like the colour. It is only the lying camera which presents an
image of dazzling white walls against a blue sky; the walls are
the colour of Cornish cream splashed with the brilliance of
bougainvillaea. I like the contrast of light and shadow. I am
excited by the grit between my toes, the first stirring of the night
breeze in my armpits, sweat cooling in the small of my back. I
am excited by Fergus. I said to him as we lay quietly satisfied,
'Why can't we stay here for ever?' He said, 'Think of the effort of
moving.'

The trouble with lotus-eaters is they don't struggle to get free.

No more now. Have just been violently sick. One drawback I
forgot to mention – the heat doesn't suit me.

Love,

Constance

My dear Sheila,

How the years fly. Here am I a year and one granddaughter later and there are you with another volume to your credit and a love affair behind you. He came and went rather quickly, didn't he, this Alistair? I seem only to have glimpsed his receding figure, running for wife and home like a scalded cat. How careless of him to forget to mention that he was a husband and father of three.

I must confess to some trepidation when confronted with *Sketches made in the course of a breakdown*. (Isn't it rather a forbidding title, or is the poetry public hooked on breakdown?) I was afraid it would be too tough for me; I hadn't expected the poems to be so funny, or so understanding of the itches of everyday life. Fergus took our copy to the lab. to show to his colleagues – a rapid translation from determined loyalty to active pride.

You should count yourself lucky. Not much pleases him lately. We have a new priest who is hand-in-glove with the Vatican and bent on dismembering the church. Cromwell had nothing in the way of zeal to compare with what Father John is doing to Our Lady of Lourdes. It's not just the idols which are crashing down along with the Latin Mass – it's flowers; only the one bunch for the Virgin, who is lucky to have kept a footing in the place. Compared with the austerity of Our Lady of Lourdes, the village church is a pagan shrine. Our young adore this man, but then he has instituted a folk Mass at which James plays the guitar. Fergus thinks the Catholic Church is running out of control.

Poor Fergus, worse is in store for him, did he but know.

Yesterday I was alone in the sitting-room. It was dusk and I was prey to that sadness which comes of waning energy. Enter Kathleen. One might almost say, Kathleen steals in, so gently did she come to me. It was so unlike her that I put out my hand and drew her down beside me as I might have done many years ago. 'What is it, pet?'

'I have something to tell you,' and she rested her head, which is the colour of bronze chrysanthemums and just as ragged nowadays, against my knee. It's not going to be a broken window this time, I thought, and I waited, my stomach cold. Then she told me she had lost her faith.

I can't take this loss of faith seriously, not when she has had it for so long; it is only mislaid, she will find it again, perhaps in the questioning later years. I listened to her earnest analysis of the shortcomings of the Catholic Church and the business of the God of the gaps and all the while I was thinking 'She is not to become a nun, after all.' When she had finished, I said, 'Perhaps what you think of as faith . . .'

'It's no use trying to wriggle round it, Ma.'

She had freed herself from something which had shackled her young spirit and felt she must be allowed to make her own explorations in the godless world. It will be a long time before we can talk about this with any hope of mutual understanding. Catholics haven't been encouraged to examine and discuss their beliefs, with the result that only too often they find rejection easier than reassessment. I said, 'So long as you don't exchange it for a political faith which is just as dogmatic and which begets bitterness and anger.'

She seemed surprised that more was not asked of her. 'I'll try.'

So she is now officially an atheist. I feel I have willed it. I scarcely know how I shall conduct myself in conversation with Fergus, who will take it hard although he will not put any pressure, intellectual or emotional, on Kathleen.

Toby is coming to stay next month. Isn't it good that he is settled, even though estate management will never pay him very well? Any chance that you can fit a visit to Sussex into your schedule of lectures? Or is next month a writing month? It is a pleasure to see your script on an envelope, but it would be even better to have a sight of the face. Think on it.

My love,
    Constance

P.S.   I can't give you Cuillane's address as she hasn't found anywhere to stay in Oxford yet. She seems to imagine that accommodation will be presented to her along with the scholarship.

Sussex
November, 1970

My dearest Sheila,

What can I say? You decree that this is not to be an occasion for sadness. They had had a long life, a good marriage and at the end they were together on that slippery road. I scarcely know what else I can offer at this moment, so overwhelmed am I by loss. In some ways they were my parents, too. I learnt more from them about family life than I ever learnt in my own home. I will try to follow your example and give thanks; but you can tell Linnie to come to me, she may weep as much as she wants here.

Of course we shall come to the funeral.

Our love and sympathy and, yes, thanksgiving –

Constance

Sussex
September, 1971

My dear Sheila,

I am in a quandary and you must come to my rescue. What is the situation between Linnie and this Indian, Pavel?

You warned me we should get into difficulties and indeed we have.

Last month Fergus's boss called on us. We are not on calling terms. Not only does he not figure in the cast of characters with which I delight my friends, he has long been relegated to the void on the rim of my mind. He is a big, gross man of the kind of which masters-at-arms used to be made. Think of any Jaunty you came across in the WRNS and imagine him twenty years on, muscle turned to flab, the boxer's face with the broken nose now crimsoned with drink, heavy jowls hanging to shoulder level. Imagine, too, that he hasn't had his teeth straightened. There you have Dr Douglas Marcus. And there we had him on our doorstep, with his lady friend, at nine o'clock of a misty September evening.

The man is unscrupulous as well as shameless. They were on their way to France and there had been trouble with the sailings from Newhaven, so they thought they would look us up. In other words, we were to provide them with a bed for the night. He has been living with this woman for years, so they no doubt regard themselves as being as good as married. 'You know Marjorie,' he said. A big, blonde woman, Marjorie is too well corseted to be blowsy, but it is touch and go. She has bold, bulbous eyes which examined me as if judging the amenities of the establishment by its proprietress.

Fergus poured drinks. She had gin and he whisky, which he downed at one gulp and held out his glass to be replenished. We left the bottle by his side while we retreated to the kitchen. Stephen was in his room studying and the walls of the house throbbed to the music so mysteriously essential to his brain processes. Cuillane was reading quietly at the kitchen table wearing ear-plugs. James, Gillian and Peg were walking the dog and Kathleen was 'out', which is the only description she is now prepared to give of her activities. I tapped Cuillane on the shoulder. 'Go into the sitting-room and be sociable to Dr Marcus and his lady friend,' I said when she was receiving me.

When she had departed, Fergus said, 'I suppose we can count ourselves lucky this has never happened before.' He was not referring to the matter of Marcus calling on us, but to the problem of having to apply our principles to people of our own age. Our children had been remarkably good in accepting our outdated moral stance; how could we change the rules for this couple? Marcus being Fergus's boss made it more difficult, rather than less, to make an exception. Compromise would be bad enough, but to compromise for what might be seen as personal advancement would really be selling out to Mammon. Fergus thought we should 'just let the evening wear on' and as I had no better suggestion, we produced sandwiches and introduced them to the children as and when they appeared.

By eleven o'clock it had become obvious that there was no question of their putting up at an hotel. Marcus had already grumbled about the expense of staying in France and she was no longer bothering to stifle her yawns. One whisky bottle was empty and we were half-way down another. Fergus has never been tolerant of people who make use of him and this behaviour put steel into his heart; I could see he was prepared to sit talking until morning. I was not. So I said, without explanation, that as it seemed late to go on the road again, we could put them up for the night if they didn't object to separate rooms. She was too startled to object and he was too far gone.

The next morning as they were leaving I asked if they were taking a long holiday. He said, 'A couple of weeks. We are on our honeymoon.' He had a gleam in his eyes, but he was not amused. Neither was I, so I said, 'If you had told us, you could have had the bridal suite.'

You see why I need to know about Linnie and Pavel. How long we shall be able to maintain our balance on this tightrope, I am not sure.

Come and see us soon if you can spare the time.

Love,

Constance

Sussex
July, 1972

My dear Sheila,

The place is the sitting-room; the light is fading. Picture your Constance as she sits alone by the window writing what has become the annual report on the Byrnes. It is one of those dark purple evenings and she knows she should switch on the lamp, the silly woman, because this is the hour and colour of her sadness. But she will sit on as the trees become dark and lose their form, the earth cools and the night-time scent of the flowers is released. She could weep with longing. So why not close the window, turn on the lamp and behave like a sensible woman? Is it bad, Sheila, to submit to this old ache, to allow it room to move in one's body? Would it be wiser, at fifty plus, to draw the blinds on the dark garden?

There. My personal social worker, Kathleen, has come in and switched on the lamp. She thinks I am one of the more vulnerable of her clients and tells me that it is bad for me to sit here mooning. A tray has been laid by my side and on it there is a cup of hot chocolate and a Danish pastry so light the Danes would be proud to own it. This is Gillian's contribution to the cheering of Mother and must be remarked upon, since Gillian is easily slighted. My girl children are in charge of me and I am left alone only because they know I am writing to you.

You will guess from all this that I have been deserted, left to cope unpartnered with the daily round of life for two weeks. Stephen, James, your Toby and Fergus are at this moment – we hope – pitching a tent in some lonely Yorkshire dale. Or perhaps on an even lonelier fell. Before setting off they had a trial run in the garden and it took forty-five minutes to get the splendid new tent off the ground. But they will manage well enough once Stephen has been forbidden to lay a hand on any of the ropes and the others have stopped arguing and accepted Toby's directions.

Peg wanted to accompany them. As stout of body as heart, she was prepared to walk her legs to stumps. The assurance that in a few years she would be a grand fell-walker was no comfort. It is the here and now of life with which Peg is concerned. She fears they will never do this trip again; it was her one opportunity to have sole care of four beloved males and she could not understand why it should be denied her for no just reason. Toby very kindly took her for a long walk on the Downs, which enabled her to make the decision to wait until her fourteenth year, a mere nine months hence. Even so, she was tearful as she watched them set off. I was surprised because when she was very young I used to doubt that this child had a tear duct.

'This chance won't come again,' she mourned.

I told her she would get over it and she gave me such an odd look, like a very old woman listening to a cradle song. Oh, the pain of youth! We say, 'She will grow out of it', but the person who will then emerge will be a different person. Youth wants the complete experience that life doesn't provide and the pain is the knowledge that every gain involves a loss. When we are older we distance ourselves from that loss, but youth knows, as it struggles towards the compromise which is maturity, that something is dying.

Enough of melancholy. As you know, Linnie came at last with Pavel – for the day. He was very quiet and I was a little in awe of him, conscious of another, older culture in which different rules apply. Fergus seems to handle this sort of situation better than I, probably because he is less aware of boundaries. James had a long talk with Pavel about Hinduism. One would have imagined, listening to them, that my son was the better in-formed. I thought Pavel was gentle with James and very patient.

I was surprised to learn that his parents disapprove of their friendship. I had always understood Hindus to be tolerant of other people's gods, but Linnie explained that it wasn't religion they were concerned about. In their eyes, she was socially inferior. 'You have to remember they were civilised when we were living up trees.'

'So it has nothing to do with the iniquities of the Raj?'

'That,' she said scornfully, 'was yesterday.'

'Will you become a Hindu if you marry him?'

'Pavel is agnostic. I think that is where I stand at present.'

I suspect she is prepared to stand wherever he happens to be. I know you are right when you say that the difference in culture is much greater than she is prepared to admit; but I sometimes feel that personality is an encumbrance she would be happy to part with.

As I looked at these young women around me, I wondered whether by the time Dominic's daughter is their age, it will be fashionable to be plump, well fed and neatly dressed, by which I mean calf-length skirts and blouses that fit. Kathleen has lost so much weight it makes her even more forceful; she has the look of a hungry hawk. Linnie, by contrast, her crumpled floral skirt trailing the ground, looked under-nourished as a Victorian waif.

But am I mistaken in discerning a certain strength of will in the line of the mouth, an inflexibility in those quiet eyes? I like to think in her very submissiveness there is a purpose, that she is saying, 'I don't choose to accept the kind of challenges which are presented to women today; I have other ideas about how life should be lived.' In spite of the objection of his parents, I would place a bet on Linnie marrying Pavel. Will you take me on?

My comforters have come to light my way to my lonely bed. We send you our love –

Constance

Sussex
June, 1973

My dear Sheila,

A book dedicated to me! This, being a collection of poems written over the years, is the book I would most wish to be particularly mine. I was afraid you might have destroyed those earlier poems which express so lucidly the feeling of our times.

Although I don't recognise what the words of 'To Constance' imply, I am moved by the picture you paint and hope that one day I may grow into a fair likeness. Did I make a great leap into the unknown all those years ago? How brave you make me sound. Certainly it was not what my mother envisaged for me. 'When you went into the Wrens I thought perhaps you might marry a sea captain and settle in some quiet place doing good in the village.' Instead, Fergus. It is his alien presence in this stolid land which has been the making of me. What contribution have I made to his life? You wouldn't care to write a poem on the subject?

Yesterday, Saturday, I stood peeling potatoes and looking out of the window at him working in his shed. He was intent on one of the processes in his beer-making, his face puckered in concentration, so lost in the glory of his creation one might have imagined him to be preparing a libation to the gods. Such a dear, familiar, unknown face. I expect I may have given him a quarter of what he needs. I hope it is enough for him to find our marriage worth preserving. The children fill my life whether I want it or not; they are there and I am here and must answer their needs. For years there wasn't much of me left over by the time I had met all those needs. During those same years Fergus was working in an environment he liked less and less. I used to get tired and bored, angry sometimes, but mostly I loved having the children to care for. Did he have as much satisfaction as I did?

It is fashionable nowadays to assume that men have a better quality of life than women. But when I read the feminist writers it seems to me that so often they are comparing the lot of all women with that of a few exceptionally gifted and highly rewarded men. Fergus isn't exceptionally gifted and I am afraid he may not have been highly rewarded; but he has given us the best years of his life and he has given cheerfully, bless him.

'Do you ever think of leaving me?' I asked him when we were in bed.

'A bit late in the day for that,' he answered absently.

'On the contrary. Some men are rediscovering their youth in their sixties, running away with women half their age.'

'And an uncomfortable time they will have in their seventies, by which time their partners may well have started thinking about rediscovering their youth. I look to you for solace in my dotage.'

It may be that faithfulness is a part of his personality. Sometimes he will drive hundreds of miles in the evening for nothing better than a change of scene. Were we to leave Sussex tomorrow he would not give it a backward glance; he has no sense of belonging in any one place. It is in his family that he puts down his roots.

Even so, I think perhaps I should take up evening classes, sharpen my mind, think up a few intelligent questions to worry at.

Forgive me that I have used the occasion of your new publication for a long screed about myself. I am so grateful to you. How I have managed to hold on to your friendship and

Fergus's love when I am so occupied with my own business is a mystery to me. Thank you, thank you, thank you.

    Love,

        Constance

My dear Sheila,

    Thank you for your letter and for writing with such warmth to Cuillane. We hardly dared to hope for an Oxford fellowship. It is a life for which she seems ideally suited and we are very happy for her.

You ask for news of the rest of the family, since you see less of my children than I see of yours. Now whose fault is that? Stephen is enjoying London, both the university and the metropolis. As far as Stephen is concerned, all new experience is good. He has an Irish girlfriend who is less than charming; the flinty-eyed type who seems always to be awaiting the call to the barricades. He still plays with the group he formed at school. How long he can continue to combine music and study, I don't know. He is not a disciplined or organised person, yet so far he has managed to hold together the multifarious threads of his life without getting them badly knotted, something of which James would be incapable. One strand in the wrong place would cause James considerable pain. He goes to teacher training college next year and already has his future career mapped out right through to the time when he will be head of a Roman Catholic comprehensive school in one of the inner cities, which he will transform by his zeal and organisational ability.

Kathleen is working at a clinic in Brighton. She brings a different young man home each month, but I fear she is so self-sufficient that all but the bravest must be daunted. Dominic, who would like to think of himself as daunting, is on the local circuit and we are honoured by his presence. He is plump, if not yet portly, and his style of speech is better suited to the courtroom than the private house. He offers advice on any subject one cares to name. He dotes on Manuela and Teresa; and there is another baby on the way.

Gillian is studying catering at the technical college. She is rather sulky at present because she and James are less close and, never having wanted the rest of us very much, she has now decided that we never wanted her.

Peg will soon be the last one at school and foresees a time will come when she is the last one at home. What will she do alone in this echoing house with no playmates, no one to tell her their troubles, to weep on her broad shoulders? Thank goodness I am beyond an age where I can do anything about that.

If you want more news about the Byrnes you have only to come for Christmas.

Love from us all,
Constance

Sussex
May, 1974

My dear Sheila,

I was just thinking that it would be too much to hope that, having spent Christmas with us, you might find time to come again this summer, when your letter arrived.

I would dearly love to stay with you for a few days, but I can't see my way clear at present. I seem to be as busy about the house as ever, only my role has changed. I am now the landlady. I leave a board up in the kitchen on which the children sign whether they will be in to supper or not, and if in, with whom. Why not come next month and add your name to the list?

In hope and with love,
Constance

MONDAY

Sheila,

The police came yesterday about Stephen. For an hour I have been staring at this paper, trying to summon the resolution to write words on it. I shan't post it – not yet. There is a fear I might harm you by association. But I have to write it down. It is like driving a car after you have been involved in an accident: you must do it quickly or you will lose your nerve. If I don't make one gesture of communication I shall be afraid to leave the house, look people in the face, speak. Also, if I don't write, my mind will continue its dreadful spiral. I am writing in the hope that if I slow the pace of my mind, impose a discipline, set things down in an orderly way, I shall make sense of events and then I shall be able to control them. When one can see a pattern, one is supposed to be able to work out the next move.

Fergus is downstairs talking to Dominic on the telephone. Dominic is in London this week. Fergus is choosing words very carefully. This is another Fergus.

The police came yesterday about Stephen. The home-based children were at the ten o'clock Mass so Fergus and I were alone. I answered the door. There were two men standing there and one of them said, 'Mrs Byrne? May we come in, please.' It was quick, yet there was time to know that something had overtaken me, I had been found out, made a fatal miscalculation. I still have this feeling that fundamentally I am at fault. No, start again. The police came yesterday about Stephen. 'Mrs Byrne? May we come in, please.' They intended to come in. I didn't examine the card one of them showed me. Their manner was their authority. Fergus came into the hall and the card-carrying man said, 'Mr Byrne? You have a son, Stephen Byrne?' Not the tone which announces an accident – more 'You have a black and white dog' followed by the accusation that the animal has ravaged a sheep.

They were in the sitting-room and we had conceded their right to be there. They conceded nothing. I have always expected people to accept that I am an honest woman and that Fergus and I are decent, good-living people. What else they think is their affair; tastes differ, I don't ask that we should be liked. But I have expected the acceptance of our honesty. It was not that proof of this might now be required which disturbed, but the sense of its being irrelevant. Their hostility was a weapon, but it was not personal. Our personal characteristics were irrelevant, we ourselves were irrelevant. We were people on the fringe of an event, of no consequence. These men did not have to bother about our self-perception, our feelings, our dignity, our right to justice; complaints to the Chief Constable were not in order in this case. Their composure was massive. Right was on their side. No, not right, right irrelevant. Facts important. Main fact, their presence. Start from that.

The police came yesterday about Stephen. They wanted information. When was Stephen last at home, how often did he come, had he brought friends with him, was there anything of his in the house . . . I wanted both to assert and deny. He is our son, this is still his home, of course he brings his friends here, leaves his belongings lying about. No, there is nothing, nothing of his here for you to paw over; never has he brought a fellow student here, particularly not a girl whose name I do not intend to recall. They wanted information yet they conveyed the impression of knowing many things, of being in possession of a large number of facts. I was afraid to form even the simplest sentence lest it collide with one of their facts. Fergus spoke to them. That chilled me, the way he spoke, looked, answered, considered, was silent. This careful man, wary of confrontation, was not Fergus. There was sweat above his lip. I was shaking inwardly, buttocks clenched hoping the shaking would not show. I clamped my teeth. Even small confrontations can make me shrill. One must never antagonise such men, the ones with mica chips set in stone faces.

The police came yesterday about Stephen. They asked questions but explained nothing. When Fergus said, 'You can at least tell us whether he has been hurt,' they asked another question. When Fergus said, 'Until we know what has happened to our son we shall not answer any more questions,' one of them said, 'You would be wise to co-operate with us, Mr Byrne.' Fergus said he must be the judge of that. They told us that Stephen was being detained for questioning in connection with the horrific incident in Guildford last week.

I could have cried with relief; this was a case of mistaken identity and soon the police would have to apologise to us. Fergus and I spoke at once. I was laughing way up at the top of my head and he was red with anger.

Then they told us that Stephen had been seen running through the streets of Guildford just after the explosion. Several people had seen him, including one witness who identified him as the drummer with a group which played that night at a private party in Guildford.

The police came yesterday about Stephen who is being held at a London police station for questioning in connection with the Guildford pub bombings. They told us . . . no, we found out, as a result of their questions, that Stephen's girlfriend has a brother in the IRA and that Stephen attended a meeting which was addressed by an IRA sympathiser. Fergus pointed out that a large number of people, including Ken Livingstone, also attended that particular meeting. They were not interested in what we had to say, other than our answers to their questions.

They asked to see Fergus's shed. 'You are Irish,' one of them said. 'And a chemist, isn't that so?' He nodded to himself. 'Irish and a chemist', much as he might have said, 'on parole and in possession of an offensive weapon'. Then, 'And you work in Surrey?' They looked at Fergus as if they were willing him to make one false move. I saw that he understood them perfectly and knew that he must suffer their insolence for Stephen's sake. Do you remember Mademoiselle at school, Sheila? How she would fly into a rage without warning? I used to think that one day she would lose her temper with me and I prepared myself for it. That was how it was with Fergus; he was dealing with a situation he had always known might arise.

He is downstairs now talking to Dominic on the telephone. I hear him saying, 'I appreciate that you know more about the

172

law; but you don't understand the position here. There is intense local feeling and the anti-Irish sentiment is not peculiar to the police. They are under a lot of pressure. I am not defending the police, Dominic, I am saying it is a very grave situation, so don't give the impression you are enjoying yourself. In fact, leave it to the solicitor . . . I am not afraid for Stephen, Dominic, I am bloody terrified!'

The police came yesterday about Stephen. No. I can't get it right. I cannot get it in the right order.

TUESDAY

They have turned the boys' room and Fergus's shed upside down. Our civil servant neighbour has called to say it is an outrage. He and Fergus had a long talk. I didn't join them. I don't feel able to meet people in case I say something which may harm Stephen. Fergus says our neighbours aren't informers, but someone informed on us about the shed. Or could it have been that policeman who came about Mrs Shipman? He didn't like Stephen. Have we an enemy there? If we have, I summoned him when I reported Mrs Shipman missing. No, that is too personal. We are not sufficiently important to be the enemy; we are people who happened to be in the wrong place at the wrong time; Fergus, an Irish chemist and working in Surrey, Stephen, his son, in Guildford and running.

News travels. Peg was asked questions at school. She has now gone for a walk with Kathleen and Gillian. James is doing something very angry in the boys' room, clearing, or cleaning, even breaking.

Dominic has been in touch with the other members of Stephen's group. They drove the van with the instruments and equipment to the hall; but Stephen seized the opportunity to call on an old girlfriend who lives locally. He has always been attracted to the idea that one can be in two places at the same time. Of course, he had not thought to announce his intention in advance and there was no one at home; by this time he was late. He ran. I don't need him to tell me, I have seen it too often. He would run oblivious of everything that was happening around him; such matters as wailing ambulances, fire engines, police cars, shattered glass and huddled groups of people would fail to arouse his curiosity once he was in the switched-off state. Even had he noticed something odd at the edge of vision, it would not have alerted him to a major incident. He is living in London where incidents of one kind or another are more common than in Guildford, Surrey.

They have released Stephen – whether because they have established that he is innocent or because they have found more promising suspects, we don't know. Fergus has gone up to London to bring him home. The children are about their daily lives. I don't like being in the house alone. It is no longer our house; it is a place that can be used in evidence against us. Father John came. When he saw he couldn't be of spiritual help, he rolled up his sleeves and tidied the shed. But there is a presence here in the house which can't be cleared away. As I move about I look for things that might betray us to the presence; that photograph album, the books in Fergus's study, an old programme of an Abbey Theatre production, the box containing your letters. Kathleen says I must not dramatise and I know she is right and I will try not to.

I think I will send this to you. I shall feel safer if it is in your hands. *Don't telephone*.

C

Sussex
October, 1974

My dear Sheila,

Linnie and Pavel came down yesterday. She told me that you have this Scottish trip planned and scarcely know whether you will be able to fulfil your engagements, you are so worried about us. One becomes very selfish in these circumstances. It had not occurred to me that this would dislocate your life. Of course you must go. There is nothing you could do here but get

174

in the way – we are all getting in one another's way. Harpo came and went when she saw the situation.

Godspeed on your journey. I will try to write to you soon.

Love,

Constance

P.S.   Dominic and Manuela have another daughter – Maria. What grief that she should be consigned to a footnote.

Sussex
November, 1974

My dear Sheila,

So much has been happening there has hardly been time to draw breath. But now there is too much time. Stephen has gone to Ireland and I need to write to you.

I must try to set this down plainly otherwise it will all jumble again like an overturned jigsaw.

The police battered down the front door of the house where Stephen lodges in the middle of the night. They had knocked on the door, but who in London would open a door at two o'clock in the morning? The landlady had pulled on her dressing-gown and was about to open an upstairs window when they broke in. This battering would have given due notice to anyone who had need to escape. The police had the back door covered, but there is a skylight on to the roof; Stephen could have gained access to the house next door had he been a desperate man. As it was, all the occupants of the house huddled, locked in the bathroom, terrified.

At the police station they took fingerprints, swabs, questioned and threatened. He had no idea of what he was accused. They asked him questions about people of whom he had never heard. He was very frightened. I think he will always be a frightened person. You wake in the middle of the night to hear someone breaking down the front door and the forces of law and order rush to your aid. You wake in the middle of the night to hear someone breaking down the front door and it is the forces of law and order. It is a different situation.

He did not seem angry or resentful, as James is on his behalf. James sees the situation with greater clarity. Stephen is too close and the picture is blurred. There is a part of his life of which he has no reliable memory. He was quiet as if he had walked into himself and closed a door. He, with whom I had had that instinctive communication which renders words unnecessary, seemed scarcely to recognise me. He looked sick and unclean; even after all our loving attentions he continued to look sick and unclean. I had no idea what was going on in his mind, but my heart told me that he would leave us. I can't believe he will cut himself off from us; though he said, 'I shall always be a foreigner in England now', that has nothing to do with us. We love him and there is nothing more important, is there? Is there? When I looked at him, I wondered whether there is something else, at this time in his life, which matters more. If so, I don't know what it is. Fergus has a better understanding of him now.

He has gone to stay with Fergus's brother and sister-in-law in Clare. The laughter has gone out of the house. Pray for him, Sheila, that no great harm may come to my darling.

    Love,
        Constance

Sussex
April, 1975

My dear Sheila,

I hadn't realised so many months had slipped by since we were together on Boxing Day. You mustn't worry about me. I am getting things into perspective. The police had to find the perpetrators of a terrible crime and there was intense pressure on them; other innocent people might have been killed had they not found the guilty people. But I have found out things I had not known, and I have learnt lessons I cannot unlearn. I have lost my faith in justice and must put my trust elsewhere, withdraw my savings, reinvest.

Yes, I would like to come to you in July. It would do me good

fear he has the unenviable gift of antagonising people of all shades of opinion.

I pray it may bring increasing delight and no harm, this search of his.

I will come to you next month. I so long to be with you.

Love,

Constance

Sussex
January, 1977

My dear Sheila,

I am so happy for you. Hooray for Linnie and Pavel! Harpo came hotfoot with the news, so before Linnie phoned we were celebrating the best news to come our way in quite a time.

It has thrown Harpo into a state of confusion. I watched with amusement while this stout, middle-aged woman juggled her precious principles in the air and finally let them come crashing to the ground. And not owing to lack of skill did they eventually elude her clutching fingers; it was the bigness of heart which dashed them to her feet. 'There will be some problems because he is coloured and nominally a Hindu.' This, I was to understand, was a plus for the union. 'But the difficulties will be all hers. She will have to sink herself in his way of life.' The feminist was momentarily brought face to face with the racial crusader, but nothing came of this potentially interesting confrontation. 'What the Hell, when they are so happy?' And there she stood before us, the Harpo of Harwich and HMS *Dipper*, eager, innocent, trusting that she would find that crock of gold at the end of the rainbow. It's not for her now and she knows it, but she still believes it is there and her joy that Linnie has found it is unbounding. She is probably the most generous person we shall ever know, Sheila.

Linnie seems to have been firm on the matter of the wedding, doesn't she? 'I told him,' she said, 'that if all his family were to be there, then all my family must come and that would include every single Byrne.' She hopes Stephen will come. I didn't want to introduce a note of sadness, so I said, 'We'll see', but I know he won't ever come back to England.

Toby came for the weekend, looking like a Viking with a handsome beard. Peg told him she didn't like it. 'It's not as if you had a weak chin.' He shaved it off. I was rather surprised.

The next time our paths cross the ground will be strewn with flowers.

Our love to you,
Constance

Sussex
May, 1977

My dear Sheila,

I hope Linnie was not too upset. He must have become a very unhappy man to have written such a letter to his daughter on the occasion of her marriage. It's not as though he had ever shown any sign of racial prejudice, is it? You are very wise. It is, as you say, as though he had expected you all to remain unchanged when he left, like those legendary figures who are turned to stone and will only be brought to life again by some great act of reconciliation. Perhaps the fact that you are all living and breathing has denied him the hope of eventually redeeming himself? I heard one of his pieces on the radio last week. Very jangled it was. The BBC pundit tied himself in knots trying to justify it.

Dominic has summoned me to London to look after Teresa and Maria when Manuela gives birth. I grumble about this, 'I didn't have parents to dash round whenever I needed an extra pair of hands.'

'Your generation had servants,' my children chorus.

'Whenever did you see a servant about the house?'

They respond with a roll-call of daily helps. 'And Grannie's generation had cooks as well.'

It is astonishing how little they seem to have picked up in the way of domestic history. 'The Wicks,' I told them, 'can trace their family back to the nineteenth century unservanted.'

'Well, Daddy's family had servants.'

'They had no gas, no electricity, intermittent water supply and nothing that could pass as heating, but they did have servants.'

They don't listen. They know best and in a few weeks (or earlier should Manuela so dispose) I shall be packed off to London, leaving Peg and Gillian to quarrel over who looks after the family.

Do you think you might come up to London to see your publisher while I am looking after Teresa and Maria? Wouldn't it be a treat to have a day out together? One is so gloriously anonymous in London.

Your hopeful
Constance

London
July, 1977

My dear Sheila,

A grandson, praise be to God! Giles to rhyme with eels, but a grandson is a grandson whatever the name.

What a glorious day we had on Wednesday. I shed years. We must meet in London again.

Love,
Constance

Sussex
November, 1977

Sheila,

I tried to get you on your friend's telephone, but there was no reply. There is no gentle way to write this. Stephen is dead, found shot in the back of the head in a field in County Clare. We don't know any more and even if we did, I can't write about it. We are flying over tomorrow. Will you think of us, please, and pray if you are able.

Love,
Constance

My dear Sheila,

We buried Stephen today in this stony little town. A triangular green outside the church, a few scrubby trees and a child's bicycle with a broken wheel lying on the grass, old men on a bench outside the pub. A grey day and cold. Rain on the wind but it came to nothing. The children were all there and Toby – did you know he meant to come? Fergus is well-nigh broken. I felt nothing much. As I looked down at the coffin I thought in a detached way that it should be me lying there. It would make more sense. The priest had recently come from Armagh. He had performed this office too many times. No words were needed between us. I am trying to keep a picture of his seamed face and hurt eyes in my mind because I have nothing of my own to store away at this time.

As we walked back through the town to Fergus's brother's house a thin drizzle started. There were pallid lights in windows. The air was raw. I wanted to go on walking but someone, I think it was Kathleen, steered me into the house. I said, 'I'd like to go down to the sea for a time' and someone said, 'There isn't any sea here.' The house is small to hold so many people, I didn't like it at all. There is sea, a longish way, perhaps, but there is sea in Clare.

We shall stay on for a few days. The children go back tomorrow, except for Cuillane. What about her college? I shall probably write to you again. It is important to fill up the day.

Love,

Constance

My dear Sheila,

We talked to the farmer who found Stephen today. He tells us that Stephen was shot in the back of the head. There were no bruises on him, his wrists hadn't been tied and there was no sign of a struggle. The police confirm this. I like to think that he died walking away from someone, as innocent as ever that his questioning might be misinterpreted. I should think that is very likely, wouldn't you? I should like to push it further than that, imagine a bright day and a smile in his eyes. Only I can't bring his face to mind. So I am left with Stephen Byrne, died of asking questions of the wrong person somewhere in County Clare.

Did I mention that Fergus's mother came? She is very old now and doesn't offer much in the way of comfort, for which I am grateful.

I have this craving for water: still, dark water. When I am in bed I think of it and then I go to sleep. Strange that one does sleep.

Oh, I forgot. We went to the field where Stephen was found, the three of us, Fergus, myself and Cuillane. A green, sodden, mournful place at this time of the year. I suddenly, very briefly, saw him lying there, head to one side, a smudge of dirt down one cheek and grass in his hair. Fergus cried. I can't. My eyes are dry and full of hot dust; it hurts when I close the lids. Cuillane's face is like a piece of blank parchment.

Tomorrow we leave.

Love,

Constance

Airborne
November, 1977

My dear Sheila,

A sunny day and the coast of Ireland beneath us, green and intricate with bays and promontories. As we were waiting to board, a man who was sitting next to me in the lounge said, 'I don't know about you, but I'll be glad to see the back of this country.'

'We are Irish,' I told him.

He was embarrassed. 'I thought *you* were English.'

'No. I am Irish.'

They have brought breakfast and when we have consumed it,

it will be the Welsh coast reaching out into the sea. Fergus doesn't eat much, Cuillane nothing at all, but I eat. It passes the time.

I have a pile of letters stacked in front of me. One must always reply to letters. I haven't replied properly to yours yet.

I still feel surprised, though why I don't know. I knew when Kennedy was assassinated that the world was a lawless place. I had hoped that being humble one might be sheltered, but there is no valid equation between anonymity and immunity.

There. We are over Wales now.

    Love,
        Constance

Sussex
June, 1978

My dear Sheila,

I have had pen and paper put in front of me. The family hover, looking pleased. This intention to write is to be encouraged. But where do I start? You have been here, your face has swum into view and disappeared again more than once over the last months. You probably know more than I do. All I recall clearly is the days just after we flew back from Ireland. 'Fergus,' I said more than once. 'Talk to me. You have talked to me all our married life; you can't stop now.' So he talked, but his heart wasn't in it.

We had our neighbours to dinner because they had been so kind and looked after the house and the animals while we were away. After they had gone I didn't have the energy to clear up. I remember sitting at the dining-room table, saying to Fergus, 'There was something wrong with that casserole.' He said, 'I thought it was all right.' He was away across the Irish Sea. We sat there looking at the cluttered table, not talking. It was that which finished me, all that crockery. Suddenly I cried out, 'He died and I wasn't there to hold him, my lovely, smiling baby.'

I don't remember much else. I seemed to sleep and wake crying, 'My baby, my baby,' and sleep again, and I noticed some of the children had come home. Then you were there. And Harpo. I was never alone. The children, friends, Fergus, there was always someone with me until one day I remember saying to Fergus, 'I haven't any intention of doing away with myself, but if I'm not let alone soon, I well may.' Suddenly it was summer and I was settled in a reclining chair on the lawn, with a blanket because I am always cold.

Fergus has something besides sorrow added to him, a constant anxiety. It will be a relief to him when I come to you. If he tells you I am very fragile still – or whatever words he finds fit – don't pay any attention. I need at least one person to be themselves with me, not a keeper, and I'd like it to be you.

Angela's mother wrote to me – you remember Angela, Dominic's erstwhile partner? She said how much she had liked Stephen and how she had envied me this lovely son. How unexpected people are.

Cuillane is watching me through the window. She has come home to tell me something but cannot find the right moment to do it. It is a beautiful day and the Downs look at their hump-backed best. I can see a spidery path and people walking up it in single file. It is a steep pull; I wonder if I shall ever do it again. There is a field dotted with grazing animals, cows, I would guess; they are too white and too big to be sheep. Did you know Harpo is afraid of cows?

Cuillane is walking across the grass towards me. Now she kneels at my side. I look at her. She has a clear skin and delicate blue shadows around the eyes; her face is fine-boned and pale and she has the look of an early Christian martyr. She needed more of my time, the time I never had; she would have rewarded long careful study. Now I must put this pen down and listen. When I am with you we will talk of what it is she has to say.

Love,

Constance

My dear Sheila,

Is it because I have for so long been turned in on myself that the light in Dorset seemed so blinding? You were exploding with energy. I felt had I touched you I should have received an electric shock. I have been reading the manuscript you gave to me, searching for clues. It is a brilliant evocation of early childhood. What a wonderful thing it is to be a writer. I had not thought the creative process so potent; in my innocence I had imagined that only physical passion could so arouse a woman.

It is intriguing to read about that part of your life before we met. Your memoirs are refreshingly different from those of so many writers, those delicate plants, inhibited at home, ill-treated at school. Here is this rough little girl, used to fighting three brothers, terrifying the pretty creatures in her kindergarten and kicking one marauding boy so hard his parents withdrew him. I can just hear Miss Addiscombe when you were presented to her together with your previous school report: 'She does seem to be something of a hooligan, but I dare say we shall be able to civilise her.'

You asked for news of the children. Cuillane has gone to Ireland. My brainy child for whom there seemed such a splendid academic future is now working in a counselling job in Dublin. Kathleen has been to see her and assures us she is all right.

Gillian is going to study in Brussels this autumn. She seems to have blotted out the past and has given herself totally to the pastry-board. James has finished his teacher training course. I don't know that he got much out of it, he isn't very talkative lately. Peg is working at an employment agency in London. It doesn't sound very interesting but she is remarkably cheerful. When she comes home she is subdued at first, but something is bubbling inside her.

Fergus was glad to have me home, but he has changed. There is a new look behind his eyes which will never go away. Occasionally, when he is laughing or arguing – which he does less now – it is masked, but as soon as his face is in repose it is back in its place. It fits in so well there must have been an empty place there waiting for it. He is doing more prison work and has become concerned about the people who were arrested for the Guildford bombing. As for me, I am much better for my months with you.

My love and many thanks,
    Constance

Sussex
December, 1978
My dear Sheila,

Don't worry. I am doing all right.

Fergus and I had a talk about his job recently. He has had to take so much time off and things are not very pleasant there. He admitted that his heart was no longer in his work.

'That has been the case for years,' I said. 'Where could you put your heart? Say, and we'll do it, whatever it is.'

I could see him in that pharmacy in a small town in Ireland. I could also see him deteriorating there, becoming one of the local bores. It was a relief when he said he preferred to keep his dreams intact.

'What is your heart in?' I persisted.

'You,' he said.

I have had to wait over thirty years for this declaration and by the time another is due I shall be dead. So I made the most of it and cried and was comforted. Later, we agreed that he should take early retirement. He does a lot of work for a prisoners' aid society and would like to do more. I know you are sceptical about the Guildford Four and what you say is true: Irish people deplore the bombings and as soon as an arrest is made they declare the police have made a mistake. But in this case there is so little evidence to justify the convictions. We must talk about it. Or better still, Fergus shall do the talking.

What about a further instalment of the recollections of a Methodist childhood?

Oh, and by the way, our civil servant neighbours came to dinner bringing with them a visitor who lives in your neck of the woods – Janice Oliver.

Love,

Constance

My dear Sheila,

In reply to your letter. Mrs Oliver, if you want it verbatim, said, picking up one of your books, 'This is our local poetess. A very strange woman. She takes nocturnal walks on the heath and lonely cottagers lock up their husbands. Our farmer neighbour has such a passion for her he runs off in the night and howls outside her window and Critchley, our gardener, who is a bit of a poacher, said he once saw them in the orchard, mother naked.'

It would be awesome to think you able to sustain this rural ravishing. Something quiet and sad, befitting one in the late autumn of life, would seem more acceptable. Is it the man I once described as a working farmer? A blunt, sturdy man, not gentry. He has an ailing wife, I believe you said.

Don't tell any more than you want. We all have things we hold close.

Poor old Potter must have been glad when I left and he no longer had to be your excuse for nocturnal walks.

Love,

Constance

My dear Sheila,

Your words spit at me from the page. All these years and had it escaped my notice that you are passionate, I prudish? True. But is there not a puritan streak of austerity in your passion? You are a bewildering person; even those who know you best can suddenly be confounded. Your poetry is tough, sharp, laconic, very much of the present time – and yet, and yet – you and this man fell in love at a Methodist prayer meeting? As I read your letter it is not a modern man and woman whom I see but characters at the turn of another century, scorched by passion, hobbled by gritty integrity. You seem to know nothing of the modern solution – pack your bags, purchase airline tickets to romantic places and leave the sick wife in the care of the welfare. Well. You have always demanded a certain scrupulousness of your men and at last you seem to have found someone as implacable as yourself; he sounds as if he is all of a piece, this Ned, hewn out of the rock of his native county. But you belong in two worlds, Sheila; it must be uncomfortable for you. And yet, I wish a little of that sterner age survived in me.

Let's not write for a while. It's the years we have in common. Time is on our side and will heal our differences.

Love,
Constance

My dearest Sheila,

You ask if you have stood in the corner long enough and may now come out. I had no idea that was where you were. It was a joy to receive your long letter. I spent the summer being rather dreary and when I thought of writing to you there seemed nothing to fill a paragraph, let alone a page.

Then, recently, quite a lot happened. Gillian is to marry a Belgian baker and we go to Brussels to meet him in February. Last week, James announced that he is to become a priest. It is not what we had ever imagined for James, but he has changed a lot since Stephen's death. It always seemed to me that his beliefs were strong, but uncomplicated – just as mine were before Suez. A few minor adjustments here and there would not do for

James. He is no pinchpenny and the new wine must have new wineskins. Fergus fears he will find the celibate life hard.

Kathleen is spending two years in Brussels studying the European approach to sociology, or something to that effect. We shall stay with her next month. She says that the baker is 'all right for Gillian'; this seems to be her assessment of most men – all right for someone else. Not much news of Peg or Cuillane (still in Dublin). Dominic and family thrive. Dominic was much affected by Stephen's death. Ever dramatic, he is now wholly devoted to the accused; there are scarcely enough rascals for Dominic to defend. He has joined the Howard League. The course of his professional life has changed but not his personality. Isn't that true of us all, though? It is the way we are looking which changes, the manner in which we apply our powers, not the powers themselves. It would be nice, though, wouldn't it? if, when this change takes place we could hand over some of our more irritating traits in exchange for ones which would make us more lovable. But no, we have to carry them with us. So with Dominic, so with me.

I expect it's too late to ask you here for Christmas, but when we return from Brussels will you come to stay with us? It seems so long since you were here.

    Love,
        Constance

Sussex
January, 1980

My dear Sheila,

You demand to know why I was dreary all summer. I am not always to write about the small change of life and keep my precious metal under lock and key. You ask if my faith has helped me or failed me. I scarcely know the answer.

My faith has not comforted me; but it has given me the assurance that this is not the end for Stephen. Don't misunderstand. I don't feel his presence. I don't look from the kitchen window and see him playing his drums on the lawn, or get a glimpse of him in a crowd, that characteristically hurrying slope; I don't suddenly catch my breath, hearing his laughter. None of these things happens. I am not caught unawares because I am never unaware. Whatever I do or say, whether I seem to attend to the preparation of a meal, listen to music, argue with the children, laugh, even, I am always aware of his death. I feel its weight whenever I move, draw breath. But that is me.

As for Stephen: when I consider all the learning, the experimenting with life which goes into the becoming of a person, I can't accept that all that remains at the end is in the nature of an endowment. 'He lives in you now; your life will be the richer,' people say, meaning to be kind. To me, these are platitudes. It is too personal, this learning that each one of us has to do; too personal for it to be some communal endeavour that lingers on after we are gone. Whatever Stephen learnt in those last years in Ireland no one knows except Stephen; that learning experience won't be passed on to anyone else, won't benefit anyone else. But I can't believe it was wasted. I believe it was a necessary part in the process of the making of Stephen, the creation of him, which still goes on. I don't think the light that was in him was snuffed out in a field in County Clare. Had I thought that I would have waded into dark water and let it close over my head. But I believe that he lives and not through me and my memories, dear though they may be to me. I believe he lives quite independently of me. So independently it gives me little joy, selfish creature that I am.

Joy I did have of him, though, in his life, and so I try not to allow my beloved son to be the means by which I am attacked by that most corrosive of agents, bitterness. Bitterness and anger seem to me futile, an ultimately irrelevant way of confronting life, like a child crying into the wind. Life is – like the river is – and we have to go with it, there isn't a choice. For me, existence is a mystery and all I can do is live the mystery. And if that sounds reconciled, it is not my meaning. I am far from reconciled.

There will be more to say one day, Sheila, but not now.

Love,

Constance

Brussels
March, 1980

TUESDAY

My dear Sheila,

It is the first time I have been abroad (I don't count Ireland) since we went to Spain and I insisted on going by boat and train so that I could see as much as possible. Zeal was rewarded by a dull, cold day. There was a violet haze in the sky as we sailed out of Dover and the sea bubbled like mercury. The ship breasted the waves leisurely and without effort; one could feel it breathing at the right moment. By the time we came into Ostend the haze had turned into altocumulus cloud and there was faint sunlight on the grey hull.

On the train we travelled between fields oozing slag-grey water. We passed a dun farmhouse with all its windows painted red; a row of white, red-tiled houses neatly squared in between low hedges; corrugated sheds, again painted red. Whereas English country buildings so often have the look of growing out of the gentle slopes of hills or crouching in the valleys, in this flat country the buildings looked to have been tossed from some passing aircraft.

We passed a small town with long avenues of poplars and a church with something like a grey chamber-pot atop its spire. There were grandiose new houses designed like small churches with stepped gables. We ran alongside a big canal and saw an enormous barge with a deck a Swordfish could have landed on. Then we were out in the country again, passing a copse with green eldritch trees with their feet in water; a trim windmill with new-looking sails like steel combs; numerous little canals and mud everywhere. Mud such as I had never seen before, so thick and heavy it would pull your boots off as you walked. It suddenly came to me that this was Flanders and I recalled how your father talked of the mud of Flanders, which seemed more intransigent an enemy than the Germans.

We stopped at Brugge, glimpsing churches with strange spires like a lot of crowns set one on top of the other. And then, at last, Brussels and Kathleen waiting, eager to greet us. She drove us through rain-wet streets, light reflected on gleaming cobbles. We passed a big square lined with old buildings of astonishingly decorative ingenuity, the rain falling in golden cascades past the lighted windows. We drove round another, smaller square with an orderly garden in the centre, the trees fiercely lopped.

'There is so little traffic,' I said. 'Is it always like this?'

'We think it gets worse daily.' She has only been here just over six months, but we are to understand that she is a resident as distinct from a visitor.

She has a one-room basement flat in a house facing one of the small squares. It is warm and clean with whitewashed walls and brilliant red heating pipes, the latter being Kathleen's own work. 'If you have to look at them, why not make them part of the décor?' A little garden, just above the level of the room, offered a reassuring glimpse of greenery. Most of the floor space was taken up with a big mattress on which Fergus and I were to sleep. She would curl up in the kitchen area, which is separated from the rest of the room by a bead curtain.

'You will see how fortunate I am,' she said in a tone which brooked no argument, 'when I take you out tomorrow.'

WEDNESDAY

I did indeed see what she meant. The square, which is near the centre of Brussels, is pleasant and in the streets running off it are bakeries and other small shops where she can buy most of her food. It would cost a small fortune to have such a well-placed room in London.

'You will have to wear flat shoes, the streets are cobbled,' she had told me before we set out after breakfast. Fergus was intent on visiting the Africa Museum. We were all to lunch with Gillian and her baker, but this morning Kathleen and I were on our own. It was soon impressed upon me that she was very much in charge of me, herself and Brussels. In the short time that she has been here her French, which was always good, has become fluent. I was not expected to make any vocal effort on my own behalf; nor was I allowed to cross a road unadvised. She treated me as if I were a frail eighty-year-old. It was touching and I soon relaxed and suffered myself to be mothered by my dear daughter.

I enjoyed exploring the many squares whose buildings offered an interesting contrast to their London counterparts. For one thing, every house is different, owing, it would seem, not to the chance of passing centuries but to individual whim. Every houseowner must have been allowed his own design; and so gables may be stepped, bell-shaped, pointed, while the distribution and style of window and balcony is delightfully haphazard. The eye lingers over details but takes away no large-scale impression. The squares are quiet; there is comparatively little traffic and no surging crowds; one can hear bird-song. Yet there is not that sense of peace which a Regency terrace can impose on the hectic London scene by virtue of the harmony of its ordered lines.

The grandiose statues represent huge golden figures bringing civilisation to brutish kneeling natives. Kathleen gave me a lecture on the subject. 'Belgium came late to nationhood and grasped what was still up for grabs with the awesome self-importance of a small country stretching beyond its means.' Having delivered herself of this statement, she went on to say, as if warning against any further indiscretion on my part, 'You will have to be careful what you say in front of Georges. He is rather touchy. Whatever you do, don't trot out any Flemish words you may have acquired.'

'Have you had arguments with Georges?' I asked when we were drinking chocolate in a café in the Grande Place.

'I try to humour him for Gillian's sake. He comes from a French-speaking area and he thinks the Flemish are only one degree more acceptable than the Moroccans.'

I listened to her talking about Georges and Gillian. 'Nothing is of any value to Gillian until she has assured herself that others covet it. I let her see that I envy her the companionship, not the spare-time loving, but the sharing of the business which is what they really pour themselves into. And I praise his bread endlessly.'

It was obvious, listening, that what Gillian really wants from Kathleen is a little adjectival inexactitude on the subject of Georges. She might as well ask for the moon.

How different we are, I thought. I talk because I love the sounds and rhythms of speech and I write because I like to see words bounce off the page. Much of the time I am not saying what I mean but rather covering my trail, hiding my thoughts, protecting my feelings; I pretend to be amused when I am angry, to be sympathetic when I am impatient, I profess to understand what confuses me and I insist that I do not understand what is perfectly clear, if unpalatable. In my darker moments, I fear that I use language not to communicate but to project to others an image of myself which suits me at that particular time. A process has gone on all my life aimed less at achieving greater lucidity than at the strengthening of a will to evade, trivialise, conceal, compromise, distort. It sometimes seems that a barrier has grown up between that depth where true feeling lies and the apparatus which processes words.

Kathleen deals straight. She has that uncompromising courage which risks losing the good opinion of others and will not give an inch to win favour. She holds nothing back, never takes cover. Anger darkens her eyes, pleasure brings a flush to her cheeks, hope trembles on her lips. Small betrayals wound her deeply; of larger betrayals I know nothing but I suspect they have been experienced. I wonder anyone can live so exposed. I am afraid she will not marry. Men get less brave as women grow stronger. My fear for her is that she will take on some quite inadequate man; despite her abrasiveness, the mothering impulse in her is strong. Why, if women are so determined to be free, do they allow themselves to be snared by this oldest of all urges?

'You are worrying about me, aren't you?' she challenged

suddenly. 'You have to have something to worry about and now you're going to settle down to a good worry about me. There is no need. I am managing.'

'My darling, I want you to do more than just manage.'

Her eyes filled with tears. I longed to comfort her, but she is one of those people who can cry and at the same time make it quite clear that no one is to come close. I remember her as a child, weeping in the garden, with all of us standing as if an unseen circle had been drawn around her inside which we must not step.

'Tell me in your own time,' I said, though I am not hopeful that she will.

Gillian has a room near the bakery. She and Georges are not living together, but they greeted us on the steps of the bakery as if they were a married couple. It was plain that she now belonged to him. He is a large, seemingly benevolent man with a dull red face and full red lips. I can see that some women might find him physically attractive. He was impeccably polite to Fergus and myself while remaining impersonal. Kathleen tells me that Belgians do not like foreigners. In my brief time here I have observed that whereas in Spain one is as much aware of the Spanish as their buildings, here in Brussels the Belgians seem strangely absent; a provincial people not at home in an international capital. This, I suspect, rather than active dislike, explained the reserve in Georges's manner.

There was nothing reserved about the meal, which consisted of a seafood hors-d'oeuvre so generous I took it to be the main course; a beef casserole which I would have expected to serve ten people; followed by delicious light, crisp waffles. Georges and Gillian loomed over us as we ate, like creatures of doubtful identity in a fairy story. I knew that I was undergoing some sort of test and that if I failed to partake fully of this meal a dreadful penalty would be exacted. Certainly, I should lose my daughter for ever. I don't know how Fergus and Kathleen felt about it, but I noticed that they, too, ate everything that was put before them. By the time coffee was served I was convinced that I should shortly die of heart failure.

Gillian and Georges showed us over the bakery and took us into the building next door which Georges has recently acquired and which will become a *pâtisserie*, serviced by Gillian. As we looked and listened I began to revise my opinion of Kathleen's attitude to Gillian and Georges. I see now how important is her praise of his bread, how heroically she answers the constant demands for approval, surprise, awe and mystification as they explain the wonders they will perform in bakery and kitchen.

We insisted on walking back to Kathleen's flat and I wished the distance twice as great. 'They won't expect you to do it again,' Kathleen assured me. 'When you see Gillian tomorrow she will be on her own and you'll be lucky if you get a croissant for lunch.'

'He seems a bit dull,' I said when we were back in her flat and I was lying on the mattress, trying not to listen to the thumping of my heart. Fergus was still walking round and round the little garden in the centre of the square. 'Do you think she will be happy with him?'

'Gillian has unplumbed depths of dullness. Together they will produce a batch of children shaped like cottage loaves.' Dullness notwithstanding, Kathleen is fond of Gillian and seems to have a need of her very stolidity. From snatches of conversation, I gather she often goes to see her sister and confides in her. It is as if Gillian provided an anchor for this restless sibling.

THURSDAY

We had hoped to go to Brugge with Gillian and Kathleen. Gillian, however, was affronted by the suggestion that she could spare the time. 'You don't take my work seriously. If I worked in an office, like Kate, you wouldn't expect me to take time off.'

I pointed out that Kathleen had, in fact, taken time off to be with us. Gillian did not hear; she has for some time suffered from selective deafness.

So Kathleen and Fergus went to Brugge and I spent the day in Gillian's tiny kitchen, watching her perform miracles at the pastry-board. A rolling-pin seems to give her self-confidence and an authority not far removed from bossiness. We talked more easily than ever before. She was a pretty child, with that curly fair hair and the big blue eyes, and now, although she is well on the way to being fat, she still retains a certain daintiness; her feet are small and those pastry-making hands are light and delicate. Her mind is as sharp as her pastry-cutters and I was surprised to find her assessment of her siblings so shrewd.

'Dom is so pushy because you were always taking him down a peg, without noticing that he wasn't many pegs high.'

'That makes me sound rather formidable.'

She didn't hear this, but went on, 'While the one who really needed to be taken down a peg was Pegeen.' I noticed that if she couldn't shorten a name, she lengthened it. 'I know you think she is the happiest natured of us all, but it's easy to be happy when one is so generally admired.'

'I never thought you noticed anyone but James.'

'You see a lot when people think you aren't looking.'

'And Kathleen? She doesn't seem very happy. Is it a man?'

'Kate can never settle for what's on offer.' She was stretching strudel pastry with a recklessness which suggested a certain brinkmanship in her approach to her art. 'I could tell at once when I met Georgio that he was the sort to marry and have a family. Kate never asks the right questions. She is hopelessly romantic and easily taken in.'

'Is he a bad lot, this man?'

Here I give you her answers and my responses. I am still too shocked to sort out my thoughts.

'You weren't all that impressed, were you?'

'Impressed by whom? There were so many.'

'Hugh, of course. That's why she came out here. To get over him.'

'Hugh?'

'Harpo's Hugh. Didn't you ever notice? She went white whenever his name was mentioned.'

'But he's years older than her, apart from being totally unsuitable.'

'He's younger than Harpo. He would have been in his late thirties when he came that Christmas. Kate was eighteen. He really is quite attractive, with that wistful, appealing look – "Help me; I'm lost and you alone can save me." Don't look so upset. He was gentle and considerate. She feels tremendously indebted to him.'

'And what, pray, did he get in return?'

'The usual thing, plus comfort and understanding.' She plaited the strudel pastry briskly. 'He told her what a bad risk he was, unable to sustain a personal relationship, doomed always to hurt those whom he loved – such as poor Harpo. I believe in taking a person at their word, but Kate thinks that if they can see the bad in themselves, they must be looking for something better. I told her, "He's insuring himself against the day when he will break your heart; then he will shake his head and say sadly that he had warned you. And you will think – another failure and I'm responsible."' She put the strudel on a baking sheet in the oven. 'And that is what happened and she was desperately grieved for him and his pain. She can't bear to think of the wasted years ahead of him.'

'How was it I knew nothing of this?' I had always imagined I was close to Kathleen.

'It started off slowly. He got one or two books that she needed and then she began to call at the shop when she was in London staying with Dom and Manny.'

'So they know about it?'

'Good Heavens, no! Dom is a terrible prude now he's married. He thought it was a matter of tracking down second-hand books. And that's all it was until some years later when it flared up. Hugh's not constituted to keep a fire burning steadily. I don't think it would have lasted long if it hadn't been for Steve's death. He was a great help to her over that.'

'She hardly ever talked to me about it.'

'It wasn't always easy at home. Sometimes we couldn't reach you and Daddy. Then, when you were able to talk about it, it wasn't the right moment for us. We couldn't even talk to one another much. Jim was always angry; if you tried to say anything he thrashed out.'

'You used to be so close to James. It must have been very hard to find you couldn't share this with him.'

'Yes, it was.' She accepted this much as she might a comment on the making of strudel pastry. I think perhaps she is one of those people who are able to discard whatever is of no further use to them.

'How do you think he will cope with the celibate life?' I asked.

'That's up to him. At least he shot his bolt before taking it on.' She answered my unspoken question. 'That silly girl, Selina.'

She was preparing to make choux pastry. I wondered whether this orgy of pastry-making was for my benefit or whether it was her daily routine. I felt very sad and yet oddly comforted by the cooking smells and the sight of the bowls and flour and eggs and butter and Gillian presiding over them, efficient as a hospital matron.

'Can I make coffee?' I asked humbly.

'There's the remains of breakfast coffee in that jug. And there are two croissants if you would pop them in the top oven.'

'We haven't talked about Cuillane,' I said when she finally sat down at the table.

'Cuil's coming over next month.' I noticed that she spoke about her brothers and sisters as if they were her possessions. I had the feeling that the centre of our family had moved to Brussels.

'No man in her life?' I asked, curious to see her reaction.

'I'd be surprised, wouldn't you?' We did not pursue this subject.

The kitchen was hot and steamy and it was late afternoon before she could be persuaded to come for a walk. I tried to tell her how pleased Fergus and I were for her, but whatever I said she wanted more. It was not enough that she was happy to have found Georges, she must be seen to be more fortunate than anyone else. 'We shan't be like Manny and Dom. She doesn't understand anything about his work. Georgio and I will share everything.' And later, 'It is much nicer living in our street than in the square where Kate is, where half the houses are let to foreigners. You might as well not be in Belgium if you are going to live in a place like that.'

.Fergus and I took Gillian and Kathleen out to a meal in the evening. Gillian chose the eating place which, she said, provided good Belgian cooking. It was indeed good. By the time we return I shall have put on half a stone in an effort to please Gillian.

FRIDAY

And all to no avail. Just as we are being so good and supportive to Gillian, Toby and Peg arrive and make this announcement which must already have gladdened your heart. 'We thought it would be marvellous to celebrate while you are here with Kathleen and Gillian,' Peg said, ignoring the fact that it was to celebrate Gillian's engagement that we had come to Brussels.

Gillian was furious. How could her union with a Belgian baker compare with the union of my daughter to your son? How indeed? Peg is unrepentant. 'I don't see why two members of the family can't be happy at the same time.' We tried to explain that Gillian might have wanted time alone with her happiness, but Peg dismissed this as selfishness.

We suggested dinner in the evening. Gillian and Georges refused to join us, which was probably as well since as far as Toby and Peg are concerned no one has ever been in love before. I note, however, that the matron already looks out of the enraptured maiden's eyes, ready to take over their lives. Do you mind Toby being taken over?

They are aware that they will not have a lot of money, but Peg informs us scornfully that money is not necessary for the raising of a large family. She talks to me as if I had never given birth. I realise that not a great deal of humour has gone into the making of this loving child; but she has other qualities to stand her in good stead. She is a natural home-maker and she is tenacious and physically very strong. Your Toby seems made in the same mould. They will become loving, devoted, rather serious parents, these children of ours; they will take their brood on walking holidays in the Himalayas, the girls and Peg pigtailed and the boys and Toby ponytailed. They will travel in a minibus through hostile terrain and we shall spend much of our time on our knees praying for their safe return. Tell me, Sheila, is this how you see their future?

Poor, poor Gillian. Or perhaps not. Although she is so resentful and can seem dissatisfied, I get the impression she is a natural *émigré* and will shed few tears amid the alien corn.

We shall have so much to talk about when next we meet. Let it be soon. Come to us next month if your schedule permits.

Fergus says I am to give his love to our in-law.

Much love from me,
Constance

Sussex
September, 1983

My dear Sheila,

You say 'No, you mustn't worry about me – not drowning but waving.' If you weren't so far out the misunderstanding would not arise. I had begun to take for granted your presence in our home over the period of Peg's marriage and the coming of Imogen, but I accept that you cannot live 'on the fringes of other people's lives'. It was stupid of me if I gave that impression; but you must know by now that you are part of the main programme, not a fringe event in our lives.

Mightn't it be nearer the truth to say that we exist on the fringe of your life? For some reason, you now find it necessary to distance yourself from your fellow creatures, be they people from the village, publishers, lifelong friends or your own children. When I read your poems – and here you speak a truth not possible in any other means of communication – I sense a shift in your perception of life. Dear Sheila, I, too, have been forced to change my own perception, limited though it is, and I shall respect your need to keep a space around you, to explore the darkness, or whatever writers do. Only don't be too rash. Remember that all those years ago Miss Addiscombe praised your tenacity in hanging on to the rock. Don't let yourself be carried out of sight of land.

In the absence of any other metaphors, I now hold my peace.

With love and a little anxiety,

Constance

My dear Sheila,

You tell me that you have always believed in accepting the gifts of life and that our friendship is one of the most precious of those gifts. This gives me great joy and the confidence to let go. I know I have a tendency to cling, and not only to people; Fergus has spent half a lifetime gently prising my fingers apart so that first one cherished principle and then another can make its escape.

You say that the last thing one has to let go is oneself. Not a very acceptable idea today, when on all sides we are told that we have a duty to find ourselves, realise ourselves, fulfil ourselves. But you are trying to get rid of a clutter of hopes and fears and ambitions, and the dependence 'more deadly than drugs' on constant anticipation of small pleasures. You see yourself as forever dancing down a path offering little inducements and bribes to an unseen person whom you wish to tempt to become the slave of the pleasures of the next moment, and the moment after that, but never of the given moment. This, I would have said, is more true of me – if not pleasure-seeking, then forever planning ahead: meals, housework, visit of children, visit to children, theatre, car service (remind Fergus), relaxation at end of day with gin and tonic. . . . Oh yes, you are right, the person who tempts, thwarts, corrupts, brazenly faces one eye to eye in the mirror.

But I am not, you say severely, to imagine you engaged in a grotesque endeavour to become a saint; and you cite as proof your continuing love for Ned. What you are doing, you would have me believe, is making a common-sense accommodation

203

with life as it has been presented to you. 'I am an OAP and certainly no one looking at me would doubt it for one moment. What has such a scarred old battleaxe to do with the cosy comforts with which the widowed ladies in the village surround themselves?' I can hear Mrs Thurrock replying, silver curls bobbing emphatically over neatly manicured hedge, 'Give yourself regular little treats, cosset yourself. And whenever you feel depressed take yourself to the hairdresser.' Life tugs you in a different direction. You are convinced that if we can only step outside the world which is limited by our own hopes and hungers, we would find a freedom awaiting us beyond all our imaginings. It may be so. I am sometimes dimly aware of its existence beyond the web I have spun for myself. Fare forward, voyager.

I like to think of you at your desk, honing words, in spring-time, the scent of blossom in the room; or sitting in the orchard in summer, shelling peas; I can bear to think of you in autumn, dead leaves crisp beneath your feet as you walk lame in the wood; but in winter I cannot reconcile myself to your isolation in that damp cottage and I recoil from the thought of the weekly shopping expeditions, you driving (badly, one has to say) that ancient car along icy roads.

If you must, you must. Should you relent, come to us for Christmas.

Love,
    Constance

Sussex
February, 1984

My dear Sheila,

I note that although I am not allowed to worry, this prohibition does not apply to you. Fergus's mother was nearly one hundred and more than ready to go. There was no cause for sadness.

Fergus and I are well. The despair which at one time threatened us seems to have spent itself; or perhaps something else has happened which we don't understand. Sufficient to say that we are close again. The silences, of which there are more, are shared and healing. I think the children find us a bit boring. They used to talk about us individually, Mother this, Father quite other; now they more often refer to us as the parents. I love having them with us, but I must admit to loving them more than ever when they are away.

Left to ourselves we should have reclined happily in some reedbank, safe from the ebb and flow of the tide. We have to thank our children for steering us firmly into the mid-stream of modern life and subverting every attempt on our part to make for calmer waters. This, of course, is what the young are for, a perpetual shot in the arm to prevent those of mature years from regressing until such time as their poor old brains wear out and they drift irreversibly into second childhood.

I go out to dinner parties and listen to some old admiral condemning all the things in modern life that aren't to my taste either and then I am amazed to hear myself holding forth in a manner which would have the complete approval of Kathleen. In the last few weeks I have heard myself advocating – no, that, Fergus says, is not the right word; I never go so far as to advocate anything, I simply question other people's advocacies. So, I have questioned the survival of marriage as an institution, the integrity of any local government officer and particularly each and every officer in the rates department, the impartiality of the Bench (of which the admiral is a member), the credentials of any party to govern; I have cast doubts on the propriety of any English court hearing a case involving an Irishman and, having become liverish on bad wine, I seem to recall hearing myself making a case for the Ayatollah.

Our spiritual adviser, James, is a curate in an East End Parish. A strange area in comparison with which Brixton (where Kathleen now works) is as English as toasted crumpets. In Brixton, Marks & Spencer carry on bravely, but here I saw only dingy cafés and dark little shops in premises which looked as if they hadn't recovered from the last bombing raid. There was a pub called The Grave Maurice with a sign, in much better condition than anything around it, representing a gentleman who would have been more comfortable hanging in the National Gallery. Nearby a period house stood isolated on an island of rubble. Side streets with splendid names, such as Greatorex Street, dwindled into dusty anonymity.

James lives in an uncomfortable, dreary presbytery overlooking a public lavatory, but it will be years, if ever, before such things worry him. He is still of an age when he expects to transform the world. Kathleen, on the other hand, now seems to have limited her ambitions to the transformation of Europe, about which she talks at some length. She visits Brussels frequently, sometimes going over for the day at the weekend. 'You are a most devoted godmother,' I told her. 'Gillian must be delighted.' She finds it difficult to accept praise when it is merited; unearned, it is intolerable. I discovered that it is not the infant Henri who draws her to Brussels but a Czech journalist with a name I suspect I must learn to pronounce.

Are you satisfied that all is well here? Am I now allowed to express a few anxieties of my own? We are delighted about the trip to America; but even Fergus was taken aback by the itinerary. Americans are cannibalistic in their attitude to writers; don't let them devour you.

We look forward to hearing about it – from your lips rather than your pen – on your return.

    Love,
        Constance

Sussex
November, 1984

My dear Sheila,

I am sorry that the past should have been lying in wait for you on your return from the New World. Toby would not speak of it, but Linnie came to see us in some distress. She and Pavel attended the memorial service, which only occasioned more distress. Did you know that she wrote to tell him of the birth of Anita, hoping he would want to see his granddaughter, but received no reply? I had imagined she had kept the newspaper cuttings for you to see, but I suppose she wanted to spare your feelings. She has never been able to accept that her mother is as tough as old boots.

I was sitting in the garden topping and tailing gooseberries when my eye happened on the words 'He was for some time married to Sheila Douglas, the poet, by whom he had two children.' This was followed by the statement that the break-up of the marriage was said by close friends (did he have any?) to have occasioned him great distress. Then came a piece about Joey, who was described as a devoted wife, surrounding him with the love and understanding his restless spirit craved. There was a long dissertation on the music, from which I gathered that musical opinion is divided, some critics preferring his later work while others consider that *Last Thoughts in the Tuileries Gardens* had a composed, lyric purity which he never again attained. Or words to that effect. Apparently, he had been ill for some years. Did you know that? Unsurprisingly, Josie nursed him devotedly throughout his final illness, during which he was prey to bouts of severe depression. The concluding words struck a chill into me. 'Those who were privileged to visit them at this time will always remember her astonishing serenity.'

I will say no more.

Before you went away you promised to stay with us on your return. You have always been good about keeping promises, so we expect to see you soon.

Love,
      Constance

Dublin
June, 1985

My dear Sheila,

You must imagine me sitting on the grass in a little park in Sandymount, not so very far from the house where Fergus and I stayed when we got engaged. The place has not changed a great deal; but I am here with my grandson – your grandson – our dear Matthew.

Our not-so-dear Imogen is investigating a trough where a stream should run but has mysteriously dried up. Matthew would like to join her. Cuillane is dealing with this situation.

'I think I'd rather you didn't do that, Imogen. Not while you've got that pretty dress on.'

'Pretty dress,' repeats Imogen approvingly.

'And you got so dusty yesterday, remember?'

'Yes, I did get dusty.' A pleasant reminiscence, this.

'And there's a lot of broken glass down there – and broken glass isn't my thing.'

A pause while Imogen studies the broken glass.

'And we don't want Matty to cut himself, do we?'

Imogen comes trotting across the grass to me. 'I didn't play in the stream today 'cos there's broken glass there and Matty might cut hisself.'

'That's a sensible girl.'

Later, she will tell Peg what a sensible girl she is; she may even tell her that broken glass isn't Cuillane's thing.

Later is when I am writing this, of course; but the present tense is so much more immediate and I want to make it immediate for you as Cuillane comes to sit beside me on the grass. We watch Imogen playing at being a grown-up in charge of Matthew; this involves much shouting and foot-stamping and the giving of orders nearly all of which begin with the word 'don't'.

'How negative we seem to children,' Cuillane observes. 'And aggressive.'

She herself has never been aggressive and I am surprised to find that she is not negative, either. She has a grave, considering face and sees no need to entertain; but she still has that lightness of mind which enables her to dance over issues that Kathleen worries at. There is a stillness within her. When I am with her she gives the impression that I can have all I need of her time; she is completely at my disposal here, sitting on the grass in a little park. I recognise this as a professional rather than a filial attitude.

'Peg is having her children very quickly, isn't she?' I say, after Imogen has been prevented from administering corporal punishment to Matthew. 'Two here and a third on the way.'

'I don't think I have ever seen anyone so happy.'

This is not said in envy. Cuillane has something which is different from happiness; that has been the really unexpected thing I have found here, this gift of which she is possessed. I used to feel she lived in the world of her scholarship; the last of my children I ever imagined working in a centre for . . . 'How do you describe your clients? Misfits, maladjusted, mentally ill . . .'

'They are people who cannot fit into, or adjust to, or see any reason to accept, what we call normal patterns of behaviour.'

She has studied for seven years while working at the centre; now she is a Jungian analyst and seems, in some ways, the most fulfilled of all my children.

'I had such dreams for you. I used to imagine myself carelessly letting drop the fact that my daughter was the warden of a women's college; I believe I even imagined you Baroness Byrne.'

'Do you mind?'

'It was a selfish dream, I can see that now.'

'All dreams are by nature selfish; we don't dream other people's dreams, do we?'

When she returns from the toilets with Matthew, I ask the question which has been so long in my mind. 'I thought of your coming here as some kind of sacrifice to Stephen. Was that silly of me?'

'Not a sacrifice. It was as though I had always been asleep and when he died, I woke up. That's all.'

There is much more than that. Qualities of love and tenderness have been released in her, tempered, I am assured by one of her colleagues, by a steely determination not to be manipulated.

'Are they manipulative, your clients?'

For the first time, she laughs. 'They are the most manipulative creatures on God's earth.'

She is no longer my child. She has separated herself from her family and, I suspect, from all personal attachments; but she has done it with such deftness that no one has been hurt, and although there is now a distance between us, it is not to be confused with emptiness; energy and brightness fill the space. My tired old heart dances in her company. But I don't understand. Fergus understands and I have an idea that you will understand; to me, it is a mystery.

I am so sorry you weren't well enough to join us. It has been a good time. I find there are no ghosts here, only young people. There has been sadness, of course; sitting on the beach where, long ago, I wrote to you about the man Fergus Byrne who promised to be rather important in my life. 'How young we were,' he said. I reminded him, 'I was twenty-six and you were going on thirty.' Stephen never got that far; but for a long time I have been trying to tell myself that it is not the distance one covers which counts and I seem to have reached a stage where I believe it.

Oh, why aren't you here? It's America that has done the damage. Gather strength; then, to make up for this cancelled visit, come to Brussels with me. I warn that Gillian is an unrelenting cook, so perhaps you should starve in preparation. Henri and Georges junior are as tubby as Tweedledum and Tweedledee.

We all send our love,
Constance

P.S.   I remember that you once said you wanted to visit the war cemeteries and I will ensure that suitable plans are made, if only you will come. But isn't John buried in Normandy?

Sussex
October, 1985

My dearest Sheila,

So, it was the man with the Red Setter. I'm glad you allowed me to stand beside you at his grave. I can't help but wonder what your life might have been had he lived; but I know you are right when you say we can't live in the land of might-have-been. Life is as it is. I will not ask any questions. There are things in my own life which have never found expression in these letters.

It was a rather tiring week. I do hope you are recovered now. Belgian food, as well as being plentiful, is rather rich.

I am glad you liked Kathleen's sombre Czech and will pass your message on to her.

Much, much love,

Constance

Sussex
March, 1986

My dear Sheila,

Dominic is to become a silk. I am sure there is a proper way to say this, but the important thing is to get it said, since your godson will expect rather a lot in the way of congratulation. A poem? You can allow yourself a little irony, he won't notice. His daughter Teresa was with us last week. Sixteen, the uncommunicable age; all over the place, like a sunburst, not centred. To think that in such a few years it will all be over, the dancing lights will go out, the stars stop shooting, the fireworks die down, and a solid young person will emerge who won't change much over the next twenty years.

Gillian gave birth to a daughter, Claudia, in January. Peg was with us last month with baby John. Did you know she was pregnant again? Gillian writes that Dominic is wrong to have had only three children over such a long period and that Peg is wrong to have had too many children in so short a time.

It seems to come at me like waves of the sea, this endless process of birth; and although it gives me joy to hold a baby in

211

my arms again, I begin to be tired. Tasks which I once did as naturally as breathing now require forethought and still they are an effort. 'I wonder if I am becoming ill,' I asked Fergus. He said, 'No, we are growing old.' Even he complains of the noise the children make. He says he has always complained, but to himself; now, with age, he feels he can be more outspoken. Dear God, is that what lies in store? A more outspoken Fergus. We have made a pact that we shan't grow old gracefully.

Oh, does it frighten you, growing old and less able and worn down by the hungry generations who are so sure we are indestructible?

I tend now to talk of a vanished, more peaceful world; but in reality it is I who have banished that world. When I fling a shawl over the TV and put my feet up on the couch and listen to music – Delius particularly – time slows down, the rhythms of life are different, and those invaders who sit in that tiny box asking important people questions on my behalf I wouldn't dream of asking, they are gone. I am aware as I listen that there is a tight knot in my stomach which, at the very first note, begins to unravel. I can feel it being drawn out from my navel; I wouldn't be surprised to see a ball of string, unwound on the floor, flowing down from me, by the time the last note of *Brigg Fair* dies away.

Peg and Toby reported finding you very tired. I recommend the music cure. If it doesn't work, you must see a doctor. Promise? This has been going on rather a long time.

My love,
      Constance

P.S.   I have just opened a letter from Kathleen. She is to marry the Czech. You were right; he is more moral than she.

My dear Sheila,

Harpo telephoned on her return from the hospital late last night. It must have been a shock for her, so she was probably a bit alarmist. I expect it is an ulcer; you haven't treated your stomach with any more consideration than the rest of your body. I thank God that Harpo was with you and acted so quickly.

I have been in touch with Linnie and Toby and we are all agreed that you must stay with one or another of us – probably here as there is more room and less noise – while you recuperate.

Should you be in hospital long, we will come down.

Our love and prayers,

Constance

My Sheila,

I suppose this is an unlucky dip we shall all have to come to, plunge our hands in the sawdust and see what we come up with. I have always dreaded that my 'prize' might be cancer, because I am such a procrastinating creature and shall need time to make adjustments; but the older I get the more I realise there are much worse things buried down there – the motor diseases and Alzheimer's. They can do so much to control cancer, can't they? And then, again, it is surprising how much of one's body one can do without. Kathleen assures me, 'You can manage perfectly well without a stomach.'

Linnie suggests we should come down at the end of the week, since you are not allowed visitors before the operation.

I pray for you all the time, as I sweep the yard and dust the sitting-room; I go to sleep praying for you.

Our love,

Constance

TO BE READ TO HER EVEN IF SHE SEEMS TO BE UNCONSCIOUS

Our darling,

Do you remember that you once said to me when I had been worrying away at the nature of belief, 'God brought me into the world and He will enable me to live my life and die my death.' I should like to add some flowery touches of my own, but that is not your way. Fergus and Toby and I are coming to join Linnie. There will be someone beside you day and night until you come through – wherever that may be.

Our dearest love,
Constance

Norfolk coast
September, 1986

Dear absent one,

There has to be a time for last words, I told myself. There has always been so much time for words; it isn't possible you should slip away, your last words written to Dominic on taking silk – 'I always knew you would go far when you showed me how to open those wretched little cream cartons with a flick of the thumb-nail.'

It seems not so very long ago that we promised ourselves to come here again and walk together on the pebble beach before we were encumbered with children. But the tide ran out before we had the time and I walked alone on the beach today, looking to where you came headlong on the donkey that morning when he wouldn't stop. I couldn't even bring you to the mind's eye.

I should like to pronounce a valediction, but what would I say? Someone spoke eloquently at the memorial service – your publisher, I believe. He painted a glowing portrait of a woman I didn't know. What kind of a life did you have? I wonder. Perhaps this is a question we should not ask. The living is all that matters.

It is midday now and I am sitting on the little stone wall that runs towards the harbour. Colour has drained away and one can hardly tell where the sea ends and the sky begins. A level light over all, the light you loved which casts no shadow. I can't take in the fact that you won't be there in that untidy study, waiting to open this in the evening, 'when it is quiet and I can have it all to myself', as you used to say.

Pray for me,
Constance

Also by Mary Hocking

A PARTICULAR PLACE

'Mary Hocking's wry straightness makes posher novels about marital unfaithfulness seem arch, pretentious and overdone by comparison' – *Observer*

'Mary Hocking is an undisguised blessing' – *Christopher Wordsworth, Guardian*

In this, her most memorable and triumphant novel to date, Mary Hocking is confirmed as the successor to Elizabeth Taylor and Barbara Pym.

The parishioners of a small West Country market town are uncertain what to make of their new Anglican vicar with his candlelit processions. And, though Michael Hoath embraces challenge, his enthusiasm is sapped by their dogged traditionalism. Moreover, Valentine's imperial temperament is more suited to the amateur dramatics she excels at than the role of vicar's wife. Their separate claims to insecurity are, for the most part, concealed and so both are surprised when Michael falls in love with a member of his congregation; a married woman, neither young nor beautiful. In tracing the effects of this unlikely attraction, Mary Hocking offers humour, sympathy and an overwhelming sense of the poignancy of human expectations.

Also of interest

FAMILY MONEY
Nina Bawden

'Few women novelists are writing better' – *Punch*

'Nina Bawden's readers should be numbered like the sands of
the sea . . . This is a wonderfully satisfying novel, wise,
tolerant, witty' – *Guardian*

Nina Bawden's latest novel, the successor to the Booker
shortlisted *Circles of Deceit*, is a tale about families, old age and
money. Fanny Pye's London house, bought many years earlier,
is now worth half a million. When she intervenes in a street
brawl and is hospitalised, her children suggest that she would be
happier in the suburbs – and thereby usefully release some
'family money'. Fanny has different views about inheritance and
property and is anyway more concerned that she cannot
remember the terrible incident in which a man died. As her
amnesia clears, Fanny realises that she is in danger . . . Here, the
tempo of a thriller is brilliantly linked with a wry examination
of the manners and morals of an acquisitive society.

THREE TIMES TABLE
Sara Maitland

'A rare blend of erudition and flamboyance' – *Sunday Times*

'Original and compelling . . . consummate storytelling . . . weaving a sensual realism across the exhilarating, fantastic myth-making' – *New Statesman & Society*

Three women – Rachel, her daughter, and her daughter's daughter – share a house, but inhabit different worlds. Fifteen-year-old Maggie flies with her dragon over the rooftops of London to a secret world; Phoebe, her mother, who has carried the values of the sixties into the harsher world of the eighties, is caught up in a private dilemma and confronts difficult truths about love and honesty; Rachel, the grandmother, an eminent paleontologist, has to reconsider the theories she has fought for throughout her professional life. Sara Maitland's remarkable novel focuses on one strange and wakeful night in which Rachel, Phoebe and Maggie find themselves facing the illusions of their own pasts. This is a powerful, magical novel about the shaping of women's lives – their work, their friendships, their mothers and fathers, the extent of their freedom and the boundaries of their experience. Rich and deeply perceptive, *Three Times Table* re-examines familiar issues and gives them a very contemporary turn.